PARANORMAL ARIZONA
MYSTERIES, MAYHEM, MURDER, AND MISCHIEF

RENEE HARPER

Schiffer
Publishing Ltd

4880 Lower Valley Road • Atglen, PA 19310

Designed by RoS
Cover design by Brenda McCallum
Type set in Cache/Chaparral Pro

ISBN: 978-0-7643-5546-2
Printed in the United States of America

Published by Schiffer Publishing, Ltd.
4880 Lower Valley Road
Atglen, PA 19310
Phone: (610) 593-1777; Fax: (610) 593-2002
E-mail: Info@schifferbooks.com
Web: www.schifferbooks.com

For our complete selection of fine books on this and related subjects, please visit our website at www.schifferbooks.com. You may also write for a free catalog.

Schiffer Publishing's titles are available at special discounts for bulk purchases for sales promotions or premiums. Special editions, including personalized covers, corporate imprints, and excerpts, can be created in large quantities for special needs. For more information, contact the publisher.

We are always looking for people to write books on new and related subjects. If you have an idea for a book, please contact us at proposals@schifferbooks.com.

THIS BOOK IS DEDICATED to everyone who has supported
me, the ghost tours, and all my creative endeavors
throughout the years.
I truly appreciate your love and support,
and would not have been able to accomplish all that I have
without you!

CONTENTS

CONTENTS

FOREWORD

I met Mrs. Renee Harper soon after I moved to Arizona. She contacted me in 2007, because she was looking for a reputable and scientifically based paranormal research team to work with. Renee wanted someone to be able to educate people and teach them how to become paranormal researchers.

She wanted me to teach people all the ins and outs of conducting an investigation from start to finish. I love teaching, so I developed a manual for her that mirrored the way I taught all my investigators. I then traveled to Tombstone, Arizona, with my team to meet her. I knew the day I met her that I wanted to work with Renee because of her professionalism, work ethic, and passion for the paranormal. I had no idea that day I was meeting someone with whom I would work for more than a decade.

It seemed odd for a scientifically based paranormal team to partner with a business that told stories about ghosts to give tourists a good scare for entertainment purposes. I was pensive about forming a partnership, because I did not want any of the credibility that my team had established put in question. I had already run into people who were using the new popularity of ghost hunting as a way to promote and bring in more business by making up stories that had no historical basis or truth to them. It was all about the good scare, so I was up front with Renee—I wanted no part of that. After speaking with Renee and asking her a plethora of questions, I found her to be as passionate about the paranormal field as I was.

Renee's passion led her to develop a successful ghost tour business, because she built it by uncovering the past with a meticulous penchant for conducting sound research practices. She stripped away the many layers buried in time and found the truths behind the lurid stories, tales of murder, and urban legends that had formed over time. She uncovered the truths behind some of Arizona's most notable cowboys, the ladies who loved them, and many other infamous characters who spent time underground mining, or just trying to survive in the harsh Arizona desert.

Lucky for us, Renee decided to share some of her research by penning her first book, *Southern Arizona's Most Haunted*, and the book you hold in your hands. Whether you are buying this book for entertainment purposes, or to use as a guidebook for your own interesting exploits, I highly recommend it. Renee has an amazing gift for storytelling, as seen by her many accolades and various awards. Inside you will find hair-raising and bone-chilling ghost stories, as well as tales of UFO encounters, bigfoot sightings, and chance meetings with shapeshifters. Sit down and buckle up, because you are in for an amazing and thoroughly researched paranormal adventure!

—**Christy Necaise**
Director
International Community for Paranormal Investigation

PREFACE

When I was asked by my publisher to write another book, I did not want to write just a ghost book: I wanted to do more about cryptozoology, UFOs, Thunderbird, and other unknown mysteries of southern Arizona.

It took me more than five years to research these stories and compile them in this book for you. Most of the stories were told to me by the people who experienced them firsthand. The people whom I interviewed were all of sound mind, though their stories seem unbelievable. Before we begin, I felt it best that I tell you the story of my little girl ghost, whom I lovingly call Charlotte.

The story begins on the Copper Queen Ghost Hunt. During the coffee and cake portion of the evening, one of the guests on the hunt asked me if I wanted a reading. We get a lot of self-proclaimed mediums on the hunts and tours, and I was in the mood for a good laugh, though it was the medium who was going to have the last one!

This woman started telling me all about my husband's family: about his mother, his brother, and his nieces, all of which was accurate. She told me of ailments my mother-in-law would suffer, all of which came true. The woman proceeded to tell me about a little girl spirit that I have with me who follows me around. She described what she looked like: brown eyes and dark curly ringlet hair that fell just past her shoulders. She was not very tall, and was said to come up to above my knee. She wore a pretty little dress with light-colored socks and Mary Jane shoes of a darker color. The woman said that the little girl's name was not coming through, yet she felt it began with a "Ch or Sh."

For all the information the woman told me, she could not tell me why I had a little girl ghost following me around. I did not tell anyone about the little girl ghost who was my unseen constant companion except my husband. My husband shrugged it off and rolled his eyes at me. I was somewhat fascinated with the idea of her and started to pay closer attention to my surroundings.

Not more then a month later, my friend Ivy, who is a sensitive (see Rita Ranch story), came by my house to visit. We were standing in my entryway and she looked over, through the kitchen to the back room, where she too saw the ghost of my little girl. She did not react, and in a very calm manner asked me who the little girl was. I asked her to describe the girl she saw. She proceeded to describe her the same way as the participant of the ghost hunt. I was shocked that someone else had seen her too and described her as looking the exact same way.

Shortly after that my friend and ghost host, Tracy, came over to help me with some projects. Tracy recounts her story of my little girl ghost:

NOT LONG AFTER I STARTED WORKING FOR THE OLD BISBEE GHOST TOUR, RENEE ASKED ME TO COME BY HER HOUSE TO WORK ON A PROJECT. ONCE I GOT THERE, SHE GAVE ME A TOUR OF HER MID-CENTURY BISBEE HOME. AS WE WENT THROUGH THE HOUSE—WHICH IS DECORATED WITH ARTWORK AND HALLOWEEN DECORATIONS (BECAUSE HALLOWEEN IS A LIFESTYLE, NOT JUST A HOLIDAY)—I KEPT GETTING A FEELING WE WERE BEING WATCHED. AT FIRST I CHALKED IT UP AS RENEE'S PETS FOLLOWING ALONG BEHIND US, CHECKING

OUT THE NEW STRANGER IN THEIR HOME. THE LONGER I WAS THERE, THOUGH, THE STRONGER THE FEELING GREW.

IT WAS AT THIS POINT I STARTED NOTICING SOMETHING FROM THE CORNER OF MY EYE PEEKING FROM AROUND CORNERS. IT WAS ABOUT THE HEIGHT OF A YOUNG CHILD, MAYBE SIX OR SEVEN YEARS OLD. AT ONE POINT, I SAW A GLIMPSE OF WHAT LOOKED LIKE DARK BROWN TO BLACK CURLS.

AS WE STARTED WORKING, I BEGAN THINKING ABOUT THE LITTLE WATCHER MORE. I THOUGHT SHE MIGHT BE A LITTLE GIRL SPIRIT THAT WE TALKED ABOUT AT ONE OF THE LOCATIONS ON THE OLD BISBEE GHOST TOUR. I THOUGHT MAYBE SHE HAD BECOME ATTACHED TO RENEE SOMEHOW. I CONCENTRATED ON HER FOR A MINUTE WHILE RENEE GOT A CALL, AND AS RENEE WAS MAKING RESERVATIONS FOR A GUEST ON THE TOUR, I GOT A PICTURE IN MY MIND OF A YOUNG GIRL.

I DESCRIBE HER AS HAVING DARK CURLS JUST PAST HER SHOULDERS AND WEARING A PALE, OLD-FASHIONED DRESS, WHITE STOCKINGS, AND LITTLE BLACK SHOES. I ASKED HER NAME IN MY MIND AND GOT THE NAME CHARLOTTE. WHEN RENEE FINISHED THE CALL, I ASKED IF SHE HAD SEEN A LITTLE GIRL HERE IN THE HOUSE. AT FIRST SHE LOOKED AT ME LIKE I WAS CRAZY, BUT AFTER THE SHOCK WORE OFF SHE THEN ASKED HOW I KNEW ABOUT HER. I TOLD RENEE WHAT I HAD EXPERIENCED AND MY THEORY OF HER BEING THE LITTLE GIRL SPIRIT FROM THE HAUNTED LOCATION ON THE OLD BISBEE GHOST TOUR.

SHE TOLD ME NO, BUT THAT I HAD JUST DESCRIBED THE EXACT SAME SPIRIT A MEDIUM ON THE COPPER QUEEN GHOST HUNT AND A PSYCHIC FRIEND HAD TOLD HER WAS FOLLOWING HER CONSTANTLY. THIS LITTLE GIRL SPIRIT HAD ATTACHED HERSELF TO RENEE FROM SOMEWHERE AND NOW I HAD ADDED A NAME.

EVERY TIME I VISIT RENEE'S HOUSE THE LITTLE GIRL'S PRESENCE GETS STRONGER AROUND US, LIKE SHE IS BECOMING USED TO ME BEING AROUND. I HAVE HEARD CHILD'S FOOTSTEPS, FELT A CHILD SIT NEXT TO ME WHEN NONE WERE AROUND, AND ONCE HEARD A LITTLE GIRL GIGGLE. WHILE WORKING WITH RENEE, I HAVE HAD THINGS MOVE THAT HAD JUST BEEN RIGHT NEXT TO ME. IT FEELS LIKE THE LITTLE GIRL IS LOOKING FOR ATTENTION, BUT DOES NOT HAVE ANY ILL INTENT.

After Tracy confirmed that maybe there was a little girl spirit that followed me, I decided to contact my friend, Jules O'Vern, who is a well-known medium. Jules confirmed that there was indeed a little girl spirit that was with me. She said that the spirit feels like I am a mother figure to her and wanted to be with me. She claimed that the number "17" was significant to the little girl in some way. She told me the little girl wanted me to be happy and to talk to her, and that our spirits go way back. Jules also stated that the girl would not age and is in her purest form. She stated that her spark loves my spark, and my dog Gizmo was not big on her spark! She also picked up that her name began with a "Sh" or "Ch" and that she liked my husband's feet.

Thus it was confirmed, as much as a ghost can be confirmed, that I had myself a little pet—perhaps daughter is the more proper word—a ghost by the name of Charlotte. In the years following her discovery toys have appeared off shelves in my home and have been found in the middle of my floor. Dog toys have been moved while my dogs were in the backyard. Toys have also been thrown off of a tall shelf and onto the floor as my husband and I are watching TV.

Items in our home will disappear and then reappear for no reason. Not to mention that Gizmo, my sixteen-year-old Shih Tzu, will sit with me in my office as I am working and growl at the door. I will tell Charlotte out loud to stop bothering Gizmo, and sure enough he will relax and go back to napping. The stray cat that lives around our home will come into my 1968 Cree Camper that I use as a studio when I am in there, sit on the couch in the back, and act as if someone is petting her. Whenever something goes array or is not working properly I will ask for Charlotte to knock off her antics, and sure enough everything will go back to normal soon after.

So now that you know about Charlotte, let us dive into some stories full of mystery, mayhem, murder, mischief, and the unknown!

ACKNOWLEDGMENTS

The amount of people who helped me with this book is truly astonishing. When I started asking my friends, family, and fans for their firsthand accounts to add to my book, my e-mail and Facebook accounts overflowed. Everyone wanted to be a part of this experience.

I would like to thank and acknowledge the following people for their help: employees at the Horseshoe Café; Karen Joy; Jules O'Vern; employees at the Gadsden Hotel; McKayla Brekhus; Robin Brekhus; the Avenue Hotel; employees at the *Douglas Dispatch* building; Clara Aguilar; Cryptid Hunter; Joe Bono; Andy at Bisbee Public Works; Caroline and Joe Gonzales; Robert Gonzales; David and Linda Smith; Jennifer Olsen; Christina Crowley; Cathe Wright; Chepes; Mark Perez; Rachel Sky; Patti, Steve, and Shane Hecksel; past employees of Daisy Mae's; Julian Roush; Sammy Hedwig; Brandyn Enfield; Ivy and Jeff Sample; Shelly, Billie, and Charaty at Old Tucson Studios; James Breen; Wade Hurst; Scary Barry; Doyle Crowley; Ceasar Fazz and the security staff at the Yuma County courthouse; Carol Engler-Foree; Kris LaBelle; Christy Necaise; Tracy Bickford; my "Boo Crew"; and all those I am pretty sure I forgot.

Also a huge thank you to my parents, who encouraged my creativity; my in-laws, who helped me purchase a new computer so this book could be completed on time; and my fur babies Gizmo, HoBo, HoneyBug, Elphaba, Madame Houdini, and Baby BambooBoo, and my quill baby Midnight.

I would also like to thank Charla Henney for proofing the book for me.

I cannot thank my husband Jimmy enough for helping me through this enormous endeavor. Not only did he help me research stories, he spent his days off traveling with me to do so, as well as helping me interview people. He is the most unselfish person I have ever met. Love you, Honey Bunny!

I wanted to give a very brief definition of some of the creatures you will encounter while reading this book. These definitions are very short and to the point, as entire books have been written about them. I just wanted to clarify what they are before you read any farther.

Bigfoot: A huge, humanoid figure also known as Sasquatch. It is believed to live in dense forests and eat mostly vegetation, though some state they eat small animals as well. In Arizona, it is sometimes referred to as the Mogollon Monster for having been seen and encountered along the Mogollon Rim. Bigfoot gets its name from the large foot impressions that have been discovered and are believed to have been left by the creatures.

Ghost: A ghost is defined as being a spirit of a deceased person that shows itself in a human likeness. Many paranormal researchers and theorists believe that human beings are made up of energy, and after we die that energy lives on in the form of ghosts. Ghosts are put into different categories, so here are just a few with their definitions:

Intelligent Ghosts/Hauntings: Ghosts or spirits that interact with humans and the space they haunt; they are believed to be able to communicate with us in one form or another.

Residual Ghosts/Hauntings: When a ghost is seen doing the same thing, in the same place, over and over again. Think of a tape recorder recording our energy at a specific event or location and then playing it back repeatedly.

Object Ghosts/Hauntings: Instead of a building or place being haunted, the ghost connects itself to a specific object. Jewelry, furniture, dolls, old weapons, etc., can all be related to object ghosts or object hauntings.

Poltergeists: A German word meaning "noisy ghost." The ghost will make noises or throw objects. Many believe that a poltergeist is not a ghost at all, but an event that usually surrounds prepubescent adolescents. The theory is that the prepubescent in the household has so much energy stored inside themselves that they make objects move without knowing it. It may also occur with adults who are going through very emotional times, such as a divorce or the loss of a loved one.

Shadow Ghosts or Shadow People: Shadow-like beings that show themselves in photos as dark forms. Usually seen out of the corner of the eye, these beings sometimes take human shape, though they have no human features.

Portals: Believed to be a passageway to our dimension that ghosts or spirits travel through.

Shapeshifter: Shapeshifters are similar to skin-walkers, as they are able to transform their physical being into another animal or creature. Inheritance, divine intervention, and the use of magic are said to be the way shapeshifting is achieved. They are prominent in mythology and folklore and famous as werewolves and vampires.

Skin-walkers: Skin-walkers are from the Navajo Native American culture and refer to an evil person or witch who can turn itself into an animal or other living creature. Usually a person from the Navajo tribe will not discuss skin-walkers with people outside their tribe.

Thunderbird: A giant bird found in many Native American cultures that is sometimes depicted on totem poles. It is believed to have mystical powers.

UFO: UFO (Unidentified Flying Object) is mostly associated with alien spacecraft, though it can be any anomaly in the sky.

Close Encounter of the 1st Kind: When you see a UFO in the sky and are able to make out specific details.

Close Encounter of the 2nd Kind: When a UFO is spotted and leaves a physical effect, such as a station being switched on a car radio or the destruction of plants in the surrounding area.

Close Encounter of the 3rd Kind: An encounter with a UFO where a being is present; for instance, an alien or humanoid.
Close Encounter of the 4th Kind: An encounter where a UFO abducts a human.

Close Encounter of the 5th Kind: An encounter where there is communication between the occupant of a UFO, most notably an alien and a human.

Witch: Believed to be a being that uses magic and spells to influence property, such as the mind and body of another human or being, against their will. Most witches are harmless and practice Wicca and Paganism. Many believe all witches are bad, which is a huge misconception.

BENSON

Benson, Arizona—a town right off Interstate 10—was founded in 1880, after the Southern Pacific Railroad came through. To this day it is a huge train town, and from anywhere in Benson you can hear the trains blow their horns to alert everyone they are passing through.

In its heyday, the mining supplies for Fairbanks, Tombstone, and Bisbee would be brought by train to Benson, where they would then be picked up and brought to the proper mine, so Benson played an important role in the mining operations of southeastern Arizona. Today Benson is home to Kartchner Caverns State Park, as well as some ghosts, not to mention The Thing. The Thing is a popular roadside attraction, with yellow billboards flooding Interstate 10 from Tucson to El Paso enticing the road traveler to take a break and discover what The Thing is. Now we would not want to ruin it for you and tell you what The Thing is; instead, you have to take Exit 322 off Interstate 10, pay the $1 admission, and discover the mystery for yourself.

HORSE SHOE CAFÉ

If you take exit 303 off Interstate 10 you will drive past an abandoned bowling alley, a Walmart, a few mom-and-pop shops, and then undoubtedly see the big neon light on the right side of the road in the shape of a horseshoe. This is the Horseshoe Café, a Benson staple. The building that houses the famous eatery was built in 1914, and is a two-story stucco that used to be a post office, bus stop, and train depot before it was turned into a restaurant, and it has remained one to this day.

My husband and I had heard the rumors that the Horseshoe Café was haunted, so after a long trip to Tucson to research stories for this book, we decided to stop at the Horseshoe Café and get a bite to eat before making the hour trip back to Bisbee. We had heard rumors the upstairs was haunted and wanted to learn more. After we ordered our food we tracked down the manager, who was more than helpful, telling us about some of the paranormal activity that had occurred in the building. She stated that bus trays would flip over for no reason; pens would come out of waitresses' aprons, levitate in front of them, then drop to the floor; her name would be whispered; shadows would be seen when the café was empty; and the creepiest of all the paranormal activity were the footsteps she would hear on the steps going upstairs.

The upstairs of the two-story building used to be a three-room apartment where the previous owner used to live. Her name was Mabel. After Mabel passed away in the apartment, they used the upstairs as a banquet hall, then decided to gut it for refurbishment, yet the project was never completed, so the upstairs was useless to rent out for events or for people to live in. It was decided the best use for it would be for storage.

One day, the manager and one of the staff were working behind the bar. The café was closed, and the only other people in the building were the busboys, or so they thought. The staircase to the upstairs is right on top of the bar. As the two were

working, they started to hear heavy footsteps coming down the stairs. Thinking a transient had perhaps snuck upstairs for a nap, the manager did not want to open the door by herself; she quickly ran to get one of the busboys to open the door with her. As they did, they discovered that no one was there. They knew it was the ghost of Mabel coming down to visit them. Since that incident they refuse to go up to the second floor by themselves; they always go in pairs.

On the day we went to research the ghost stories, the manager was nice enough to let us (and a very curious patron sitting in the booth behind us who overheard our conversation) go into the back to view the haunted staircase. At the time I was using a knee scooter due to tendonitis in my foot. I left the scooter beside the door in the bar—a good five or six feet away—and hobbled back to the staircase to take photos and hopefully witness a dark shadow moving across the top of the stairs.

We finished taking our photos and tried to open the door leading back to the bar, but something was obstructing the door. The manager gave it a hard push and

Staircase leading to the second floor of the Horse Shoe Café.
Author Photo

Inside the bar area of the Horse Shoe Café. *Author Photo*

the door finally opened. What we discovered was that someone or something had pushed my scooter from its place in front of the door to prevent us from leaving. Mabel must be lonely and wanted someone to scare up a conversation with!

Or perhaps there is more to the hauntings at the Horseshoe Café.

Before Benson was turned into an actual city, it was run by posses who would capture outlaws and hang them in the old lumber yard, which is where the Horseshoe Café now stands. Due to trees not being big enough or strong enough to hang men, the posses used the beams in the lumberyard as a makeshift gallows.

One of the most interesting stories in Benson folklore involves three men who were hanged in the lumberyard and are now said to haunt the old Benson Pioneer Cemetery. The story is called the "Los Tiraditos Legend."

In the 1880s, a train that had stopped in Benson was the target of a train robbery by two men. Around the same time a horse was stolen by another individual. Three strange men from Mexico who were new in town, who might or might not have been the ones who committed these crimes, were apprehended and found guilty. With no sheriff, no law, no judge, and no jury, it was decided by the posse that these three men should hang until dead, and so it was done.

Their coffins were made out of wood from the lumber yard and they were carried to the cemetery. It was decided that these men should not be buried in "hallowed ground" with the good, upstanding, deceased townsfolk, but rather outside the cemetery grounds in a potter's grave, where they would not share the same ground as good, law-abiding people. Their graves were marked with three wooden crosses constructed with wood from the same lumberyard where they met their keeper.

Over the years a natural wash separated the graves from the cemetery even more, though many would pay their respects by bringing candles, food, flowers, and other offerings to the grave site of these so-called criminals. Many of the townsfolk felt that the men were innocent and there was no proof that they had committed the crimes, and that they belonged within the cemetery walls. Wax from the candles that had been brought to honor their souls was found in trees nearby. All Saints Day proved to be a day the men were not forgotten, as their graves were always cleaned and offerings were always brought.

After one hundred years the bodies were finally exhumed from their graves and reburied within the Benson Pioneer Cemetery walls. Three metal crosses on the ground and a few plaques depicting the legend indicate where the bodies were moved.

The locals will tell you that the souls of these three men are still not at peace. Late at night residents have claimed to hear screams and creepy wailing coming from the location of their original graves. Others have claimed to see the ghosts of men hanging in midair in the cemetery.

SKIN-WALKERS AT TRIANGLE T RANCH

Triangle T Ranch is right off I-10, not very far from Benson. The ranch is nestled among the strange and unique rock formations that make up the Dragoon Mountains, a must-see destination for anyone visiting southeastern Arizona.

Triangle T Ranch was founded in 1922, and boasts being the second oldest ranch in the entire state. The property consists of eleven guest rooms and has 162 acres for guests to explore. It is most famous for its horse trails with scenic views, and also has an old-fashioned Wild West-styled saloon. The ranch was a very popular destination for celebrities like Steve McQueen, Clark Gable, Gregory Peck, Will Rogers, and John Wayne, as well as for wealthy families like the Rockefellers and Vanderbilts. Also situated on the property is one of the original movie sets from the movie *310 to Yuma* with Glen Ford.

Where Triangle T Ranch sits is right in the heart of land frequented by Navajo Athapaskons that migrated south from Canada in the 1300s. The ones who settled in Arizona and New Mexico became known as the Apache tribe. The Native Americans brought many traditions and superstitions, including that of skin-walkers.

Skin-walkers are believed to be magical creatures that walk among the Native American tribes. These beings are able to transform themselves under the cover of darkness from human form into animal form. Skin-walkers are believed to have

Benson Pioneer Cemetery. *Author Photo*

The graves of the men involved in the Los Tiraditos Legend inside Benson Pioneer Cemetery. *Author Photo*

reached the highest level of priesthood within their tribes and are always the tribes' medicine men. To become a skin-walker they must kill a member of their family, turning them into an evil soul. The animals into which skin-walkers are able to transform include coyotes, crows, owls, bears, and wolves. Skin-walkers are believed to be able to read minds, and therefore discover a person's deepest, darkest fears, using those fears to their advantage.

Many people have reported seeing skin-walkers running at up to sixty miles per hour alongside their cars, tapping on their windows, and then vanishing into the night. They also peer into windows of homes and buildings, looking for people to manipulate. They have been known to appear in people's dreams and somehow manipulate their dreams.

My friend Karen had what she believed to be a skin-walker experience while staying at Triangle T Ranch in April 2016. She claims she was visited by what she believed to be a skin-walker. She saw a huge black mass that she described as "blacker than black," and felt what she described as "one hundred souls all crowded together and unhappy in a small fenced area behind the pool and bar."

When she went walking on the rock formations around the ranch she stated that at some points she felt her legs and feet were lead and pulling toward the rocks, though at other times she felt light as a feather, as if the wind was going to blow her away. It was a strange sensation that she felt and was surely paranormal. At night, she saw a woman with kind eyes but no other facial expression in her room by the window. Karen states that she was sleeping, but felt she was awake at the same time. She tried to call out to her roommate but was unable to speak. The woman at her window was outside the room, but Karen could tell that she was illuminated in an icy bluish-white glow and her hair was platinum colored. The woman held an ice blue glowing ball in her hands that almost matched the glow illuminating her body.

The woman set the glowing ball on the windowsill of Karen's room and then she put another light in the room's dresser through a closed and locked window. When Karen awoke, her roommate and her roommate's mother asked her what she was talking about at around four a.m. They claimed that in a calm voice Karen said, "Something weird is happening." April—Karen's sweet and gentle pit bull—was sleeping on Karen's bed that night and got up at the same time Karen was seeing the strange woman. April went to wake up the roommate and her mother in time for them to hear Karen talking in her sleep. Did April sense the strange spirit woman's presence?

Karen decided to research who this woman was that visited her. She discovered that near the site of Triangle T Ranch was a winter haven for Native Americans, and an internment camp where their women and children were slaughtered. In her research, she found that it might have been a spirit or a Haniel that comes to protect the intuitives and empaths from bad spirits attacking them. Considering that this experience happened the night after Karen felt the negative energy and black mass behind the pool and bar, was the woman Karen saw an archangel that was protecting her from a skin-walker? Or was it a skin-walker disguising itself as a protector to get access to Karen? Or did Karen experience a shadow ghost? Perhaps it was just a bad dream . .

Douglas, Arizona, sits on the American/Mexican border, and was officially founded in 1901, and incorporated in 1905. Douglas was a sleepy border town with some cattle ranches until the copper mines of Bisbee, Arizona—some twenty-seven miles away—needed smelter facilities for their copper ore.

During Douglas's heyday there were two copper smelters in town, but both were taken down after the copper mines of Bisbee closed and they were no longer needed. Today Douglas is a sleepy little town, with many of its residents being of Mexican/Latino descent.

Douglas was put on the map in 1926, when evangelist Aimee Semple McPherson was found in Agua Prieta—the town bordering Douglas in Mexico—and brought to Douglas to be hospitalized. She was thought to have drowned at a beach in Los Angeles, but had really been kidnapped, tortured, and then escaped. It made the news all over the world, and Douglas openly received reporters, photographers, and curious individuals who wanted to visit where the minister sought refuge.

Today Douglas is filled with adorable Victorian and Craftsman style homes that throw you back to a time when it was a booming town. Many people do not bother to visit, though they should. Douglas is home to a museum filled with art cars known as Art Car World, featuring forty-two art cars—including "Cathedral," the art car hearse. It is also home to the "Water Heater Virgin Mary."

At the corner of 6th Street and G Avenue sits a white house with pink curtains. On the side there is a little glass house attached to the main house. Inside this enclosure sits a rusting water heater. Some claim the rust forms an image of the Virgin Mary. The locals will place candles and pictures of loved ones in the glass house to ensure prayers from the virgin mother. When I went, I saw a blob of rust and could not make out the Virgin Mary for the life of me, but nonetheless, it is definitely worth checking out if you are in the area visiting some of the local ghosts, which there is no shortage of.

THE GADSDEN

The Gadsden Hotel is the jewel of Douglas, Arizona. The original building was constructed in 1907, and was one of the most elegant, extravagant hotels in Arizona. In 1929, the hotel had to be rebuilt after a fire destroyed all of the building except for the marble staircase. When it was rebuilt, they added Tiffany stained glass murals, stained glass skylights, and gold leaf capitals that sit on the four marble columns in the lobby.

When you walk into the Gadsden, you are immediately taken to a time in history that no longer exists: a time when cattlemen, ranchers, and businessmen would fill the hotel with card games, business deals, and talk of all the opportunities the vast countryside had to offer.

The Gadsden is full of stories about the paranormal. Robin Brekhus used to be the manager and has a plethora of ghost stories about the building. Her in-laws

Some Douglas residents believe the image of the Virgin Mary made of rust is on this water heater. There is now a protected shrine to the virgin mother at this residence. *Author Photo*

purchased the neglected building in 1988, and since then the ghosts have made their presence known to Brekhus and her family, who for a long time lived in the hotel.

One of the most familiar ghost stories of the Gadsden occurred on Friday the thirteenth in March 1991. The electricity had gone out in the building and Robin had to go into the basement to get candles. As she was walking through the maze of hallways making up the basement, she saw a misty fog in the shape of a human body. She could not make out any details of the figure.

Past and current employees of the hotel do not like to go into the basement for fear of encountering the ghost that lurks there. One employee told us that he was in the basement area cleaning rat traps when he felt someone behind him and saw a foggy figure out of the corner of his eye.

One might wonder why a disembodied spirit would haunt a dark and dingy basement of an old hotel. One of the many folklore stories of the hotel might hold the answer. It is believed that someone in the heyday of the hotel, or perhaps during the Depression, buried gold under the building. They never disclosed where the gold was buried. Of course there is no proof that this happened, and this is a story told in many haunted buildings in Arizona (per my chapter on Big Nose Kate's in *Southern Arizona's Most Haunted*), but many of the hotel's employees believe that the ghost in the basement is searching for the long-lost gold.

There are many other ghosts that are believed to haunt the historic hotel.

Robin Brekhus's daughter McKayla would play with the hotel's little boy ghost in the mezzanine of the building. She recounts that when she was between ages three and seven she would play with the ghost of a little Native American boy. McKayla was somewhat of a tomboy when she was a child and preferred to play with toy cars rather than dolls. She remembers thinking that her ghostly friend was

Outside the haunted Gadsden Hotel in Douglas, Arizona. *Author Photo*

The grand staircase in the Gadsden Hotel.
Author Photo

no different than any of the other friends she had, except that she was the only one who could see him. Her brother never saw him, only her.

She remembers one day playing with some toy cars, then losing interest and starting to play with another toy, when the toy car started to move across the floor by itself. She also remembers one day building a structure out of Legos with her brother. All of a sudden the toy building crashed to the floor and was destroyed. McKayla believes the ghost of the little boy destroyed her masterpiece. After she turned seven the ghost of the little boy stopped showing himself to McKayla and she was very saddened by his disappearance.

McKayla was told that the little boy had fallen off the mezzanine onto the floor of the lobby, which is how he passed, and that he haunted the mezzanine in search of children to play with. Many guests who visit the Gadsden Hotel will leave toys and trinkets for the little boy ghost to play with. Sometimes these objects actually disappear, never to be found.

There is also the ghost of Everette "Matt" Matthews, who used to frequent the Gadsden almost every day. He would sit in the coffee shop attached to the lobby, socialize with his friends, and flirt with the women. This was Matthews's daily ritual for more than ten years. On April 25, 1991, Matthews passed away of a heart attack, though his spirit is believed to still be at the small coffee shop at the Gadsden.

After his passing, Matthews's friends would recount stories to his family about seeing his spirit walk into the café and sit down for a cup of coffee. A friend of Matthews's daughter-in-law saw his ghost walk into the coffee shop, but did not know it was a ghost. She wanted to sit and have a chat with Matthews but did not have the time. Later that evening she called his daughter-in-law's house asking to speak with him, and they informed her he had passed away a few weeks prior.

Matthews also haunts his family's home every year around the anniversary of his death. Doors will open for no reason, light bulbs will pop and have to be replaced, and electronic equipment will turn on by itself. When the family members acknowledge his spirit being present and call out his name the paranormal activity will stop for the rest of the day, but sometimes starts all over again the following day.

Of all 160 rooms of the Gadsden Hotel, room 333 is supposed to be the most haunted. Guests have had the lights in the room turn on and off by themselves, the bed shakes, and there are claw marks on the door. The maintenance staff will paint over the scratch marks and a few days later they reappear.

Guests have also claimed to see an indentation on the bed, as if someone is sitting next to them. Others have claimed ghostly figures have gotten into bed with them while staying in the room. Once when a guest was opening the door to room 333 all the lights in the third floor hallway turned off. Shoes will be moved from one end of the room to the other, and weird scents are smelled, from freshly baked

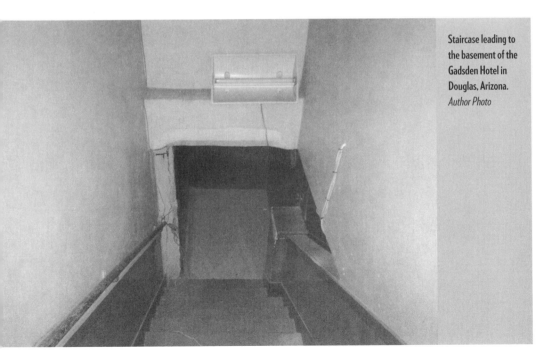

Staircase leading to the basement of the Gadsden Hotel in Douglas, Arizona. *Author Photo*

Door to room 333, believed to be the most haunted room at the Gadsden Hotel in Douglas, Arizona. *Author Photo*

cake to sulfur. No one is certain who the ghost is that haunts room 333. Maybe you should take a visit to the Gadsden and ask for Room 333 to find out for yourself.

Avenue Hotel

The Avenue Hotel that sits on G Avenue in Douglas near the old train station was once a thriving hotel, bar, and restaurant that catered to the traveling railroad employees who would come through Douglas on their way to the next big city. The original building was built in 1901, and the south side addition was constructed in 1915. As the mining industry declined, so did the Avenue Hotel. It stood vacant for the most part since 1975, until Henry and Robin Brekhus purchased it. Robin, who is the manager of the Gadsden Hotel, loved the building, and was hoping to one day open up a bed and breakfast. The family moved in shortly after acquiring the home, and soon the ghost made its presence known.

The ghost is said to be that of Mabel McGee. Mabel lived and worked at the hotel, most likely as a saloon girl. She had a son, but the father of her child is unknown. Believed to have been married to a man by the name Alfonso, it is reported that she had a few lovers while her husband was away.

On March 14, 1905, at the tender age of eighteen, Mabel died from an apparent drug overdose, though some speculate that she was murdered by her husband. Many believe that her husband wanted Mabel and her son to move with him to California; Mabel refused, and this made her husband irate. He then murdered her and left town.

Whether it was a drug overdose or foul play, Mabel's disembodied spirit still haunts the Avenue Hotel and seems to watch over its residents.

Shortly after moving into the building, McKayla Brekhus, Robin's daughter, had some friends over and they were playing Garage Band at around 6 p.m. one evening. All of a sudden they started hearing banging noises coming from upstairs. They followed the noises to Mabel's old bedroom. When they opened the door, they were surprised to see their moving boxes that had been piled in the room to be sorted through falling to the floor. They went to leave the room and the door locked itself. When they got it opened, they ran downstairs to the bar area. Once they reached the bar they started to hear a female voice. They decided to go back upstairs to discover where the voice was coming from, and they followed it back to what used to be Mabel's room. As they approached the room the door slammed closed.

McKayla eventually turned Mabel's room into her own bedroom. On McKayla's eighteenth birthday, she awoke at 4 a.m. to the door rattling and the electricity in the room turning off. Out loud McKayla said, "I am all right Mabel," to assure Mabel that she was not going to succumb to the same fate that Mabel did. Right after McKayla made the verbal reassurance everything turned back on. Their dog Luna started barking at the closet door, and it was then that McKayla discovered an old vintage birthday card that had slid from inside the closet, under the closet door, and onto the floor of her bedroom.

Outside the haunted Avenue Hotel in Douglas, Arizona. *Author Photo*

The day after her birthday McKayla told us that her bedroom door would not open right away, her hair dryer would not work, and there was no hot water when she wanted to take a shower. Was this Mabel's way of showing McKayla that she is still there, watching her to make sure that everything was OK and to make sure that nothing bad happens to her?

DOUGLAS DISPATCH BUILDING

On quiet 11th Street, off the main drag in downtown Douglas, sits the *Douglas Dispatch* building. The building's original purpose was as a mortuary, but soon the local paper moved in.

Employees of the *Dispatch* claim that the building is haunted. They believe the spirit of the former owner, Andrew Loney, haunts the building. Loney owned the newspaper for a number of years. He would walk miles to work every day instead of driving or taking public transportation. He also took a very hands-on approach to running the business, helping in every department. His coworkers stated he was a very quiet yet hardworking individual who cared a lot for his businesses and the city of Douglas.

So it is no surprise that many of the employees at the *Douglas Dispatch* believe that its resident ghost is Andrew Loney. His spirit is said to be felt mostly in the old press room, as well as in the receptionist area. The former receptionist had a guest walk into the office one afternoon and immediately start screaming. The receptionist asked what was wrong and the guest responded that there was a ghostly apparition of a man standing behind her.

Employees claim to hear strange noises, and have papers and objects move about the office. All agree that the ghost does not seem scary and have coined it the "Night Watchman," because it appears to be looking over the business and the employees to make sure everything is running smoothly.

ROUTE 666

Believed to be a cursed stretch of highway spanning over 200 miles, the formerly named Route 666 runs right through Douglas, Arizona. Arizona was the first state to rename Route 666 to Route 191, after receiving years of complaints from people who refused to drive on this stretch of highway because they thought the highway's numerical number was associated with the Devil.[*]

Though the number has been changed, many still refuse to drive on the desolate stretch of road due to the tales of accidents occurring there, bad luck to drivers who had recently driven on it, and the abundance of paranormal activity experienced by thousands of people who have driven the lonely highway.

Many individuals claim to have been run off the road by a huge trailer truck that appears to be on fire and heading straight toward them. Many state that this fiery truck will drive from one end of the highway to the other, causing numerous one-car accidents.

Another common story involves drivers who get out of their car to stretch their legs or relieve themselves. Often they will see and hear a pack of vicious, wild dogs called hounds of hell. When the individuals get back in their car and start driving off the dogs run after them, just as fast as the car. Many of Route 666's accidents are blamed on these animals, which are believed to be able to shred tires with their claws and teeth.

Some people also claim to see the ghost of a woman dressed all in white walking alongside the road. This is known in ghost folklore as a hitchhiking ghost and is a common folklore ghost story. The strange thing about the hitchhiking ghost on Route 666 is that the same motorist will see her numerous times on different stretches of the road.

Shapeshifters have also been known to frequent the stretch of highway. The stories involving these creatures on Route 666 usually have them sneaking into the back seat of a car as a fly and then shifting into a different animal to scare the driver,

---

[*]Revelation 13:18 states: "Let him who has understanding calculate the number of the beast, for it is the number of a man: His number is 666."

forcing them to have an accident. Shapeshifters are also believed to cause accidents by appearing in front of oncoming cars in the middle of the road. Witnesses say the animals appear out of nowhere.

Time loss is also not uncommon along this stretch of the "Devil's Highway." People have gone missing and then reappeared on the highway, not able to remember where they were or for how long. The same thing has happened to people walking alongside the road who disappear without a trace, then reappear miles away from where they were last seen. They do not know or remember how they got to where they were or how long they were gone.

My friend Clara lived in Douglas when she was younger and recounted much of the common folklore regarding the old highway. One night Clara's mother decided to take Route 666. Upon turning on to the street her car died. She got it to start again and decided since she was alone to turn around and go home. Her car worked fine after that occurrence, and she blames the haunted highway for making her car die. This occurrence gave some validity to the stories Clara had been told about the haunted stretch of highway and the bad luck it can inflict on travelers.

My husband and I experienced some of this so-called bad luck ourselves after driving on the haunted stretch of road. While taking photos for this book, my husband and I took a ride down Route 666. It seemed pleasant enough, until we came to an old cemetery. We decided to get out and look around. The cemetery was in disarray. Some of the graves had wooden crosses with names and dates that were barely legible. In other parts there were unmarked graves, but you knew someone was buried underneath because of the mound of dirt. Some had tombstones that were more recent, as if someone was trying to refurbish the old graves.

It was a creepy place, yet fascinating for anyone who likes to frequent old cemeteries. As we started to walk around we got an uneasy feeling, as if being watched by eyes in the nearby dessert brush. When the wind blew we could have sworn we heard voices, yet we were all alone—just us, the road, and the lost souls buried six feet below. An uneasy feeling came over us and we decided to head back to the car.

We drove back to Douglas and to my husband's work, where they were having a blood drive. My husband gives blood multiple times a year and has never had a problem. When he went to give blood after driving down Route 666 his good luck changed. I was with him in the bloodmobile and could tell something was wrong when the nurse could not find a vein. Another nurse came over and started screaming. My husband had fainted, even before they were able to get the needle in his arm. After he came to he did not know where he was or what had happened.

Immediately afterward I got an uneasy feeling and had to leave the bloodmobile. I felt sick and faint as well. I got a bottle of water and sat for a half hour until the sickening feeling passed. At this point we decided that driving down Route 666 was a bad idea, that the stories of bad luck occurring to drivers who have taken the road were true, and that we would never do it again.

Route 666 cemetery in Douglas, Arizona. *Author Photo*

FLYING OBJECTS OVER DOUGLAS

Much like most cities in southern Arizona, Douglas has its fair share of UFO sightings. Being in such a desolate area and sitting right on the Mexico border, with no big cities within a two-hour drive, it is no wonder flying saucers frequent the area.

Documented sightings in Douglas date to 1947, when a woman who was looking south, in the direction of Mexico, saw a spherically-shaped UFO that was completely illuminated. She watched it lift off the ground into the air and then vanish among the stars.

There is a story of a grandmother and her granddaughter who were driving home from church in the early afternoon when they saw an object overhead. They claimed the object had flashing lights and was flying in a circular pattern. At the time it was happening they tried to call family members to tell them, but were unable to due to the cell phone reception having too much static. Could the flying saucer they saw have been interfering with their cell reception?

A friend of mine was driving alone down Double Adobe Road towards Central around 9:30 p.m. when she looked up in the sky and saw a circular group of lights hovering and chasing each other over Douglas. She described them as oval in shape, pale, and moving quickly. She thought at first they might be helicopters, then realized that they could not be helicopters, because they were in the clouds and moving unlike any helicopter she had ever seen.

The most famous UFO sighting in Douglas is the Phoenix Lights, prior to them reaching Phoenix. On March 13, 1997, there were numerous sightings of unidentified flying objects in Arizona, Nevada, and Sonora, Mexico. Thousands of people witnessed strange lights in the sky that evening. The objects had six lights in a triangular formation that moved slowly through the sky. It made national headlines, and much research can be done on this strange occurrence.

That same evening in Douglas people were witnessing the strange UFOs across the Southwest; a triangular craft was seen flying over the city north toward Phoenix by radio tower 70. Witnesses claim it was huge, moved extremely slowly, and blocked out the stars in the sky. All that could be seen were the lights from the object.

THE DOUGLAS WITCH

Almost every small town in America has folklore regarding the town witch that is typically told on the full moon at sleepover parties, around campfires, or just around the water cooler on Halloween. Douglas, Arizona, is no exception.

There is the story about Bess Shapiro, who was born in 1910, in El Paso, Texas, and lived most of her life in Douglas. As the folklore goes, she was believed to have been a witch. Not a good witch, but a bad witch, who would practice black magic in secrecy, casting evil spells among those who did her wrong. One night she was discovered by a local practicing her witchcraft. It was not long before word got around town about her living a secret life as a witch and the townspeople of Douglas were infuriated.

On Halloween night 1963, it is believed that the local townspeople went to the Shapiro house after Bess had gone to sleep. They set her home on fire, burning her alive inside. She was buried a few days later in the Jewish section of the Douglas Cemetery. Many say that if you go to her grave on a full moon—especially if the full moon is on Halloween night—and watch from a distance, you can see her ghost walk out of her plot and start dancing among the other graves. They warn you to not be caught watching her or she will take your soul and curse your spirit for eternity.

Pretty good story, huh? Well, if you ask the city of Douglas, or if you do some deep research into Bess Shapiro, you will discover that they claim she passed away in Long Beach, California, of natural causes. You will also discover that she was married to a doctor and had a son and daughter. If you ask locals from Douglas, they will tell you that the story of her passing away in her home in Long Beach was a fabrication to hide the fact that the city of Douglas was involved with the burning of her home and the ultimate death of Mrs. Shapiro.

There is one very important piece of information to ponder that might support the fact that she did indeed pass away in Douglas. Since Bess Shapiro was buried in the Jewish section of the Douglas cemetery, it is safe to assume she was a practicing Jew. According to Jewish law, after death the body must be put in the ground as soon as possible; within a day or two is customary. It is strictly forbidden to embalm

The location where the Douglas witch house used to be. *Author Photo*

the body in Jewish law. Therefore, if Bess Shapiro was living in Long Beach, it would have been nearly impossible to transport her body back to Douglas for her funeral in the allotted amount of time according to Jewish law without having her embalmed. Also, why would they not have simply buried her in California? Why would they have paid the expenses to have her body brought back to Douglas instead of having her buried in California, where it is believed that her family resided, including her children and siblings? She also has no deceased relatives in the Douglas Cemetery except for her husband, who was believed to have died a few years after her, also on Halloween night.

We will let our readers choose which story they wish to believe.

Bess Shapiro's story is not the only one related to witches in Douglas. On July 17, 1912, the *Arizona Daily Star* published an article about a witch trial that took place in the border town. Mr. and Mrs. Jesus Belara lived on 11th Street, between F and H Avenues, with their five-year-old daughter. Their daughter was suffering from an eye infection that her parents believed was caused by their neighbor, Petra Tautines. They claimed that Tautines put an evil spell on their daughter, causing the infection.

Tautines denied that any witchcraft was performed on the child and filed a countersuit in court, claiming that Mr. Belara had hit her. The judge brought in Dr. E. W. Adamson, who was treating the Belara girl's eye infection, and he testified the girl was suffering from an ordinary infection. Thus Tautines was not charged with the act of witchcraft.

CHAPTER 2

Skin-walkers Near Douglas

The following story was told to me by Cryptid Hunter from Strange World Paranormal. It takes place along the Arizona and New Mexico border, which is why I added it to the Douglas section of this book. As far as I can tell Douglas is the closest city to where the story takes place, though it is uncertain due to the references Cryptid Hunter makes to a small village or town; at the time Douglas would have been much larger than it is today. Either way, it is an interesting story like no other.

The man who related the story to Cryptid Hunter is part Navajo. He was in his late eighties when he told about his experience. When he was younger, his father would often send him to take care of their sheep out in the field. Sometimes he had to walk miles to go find them, and occasionally, when a sheep got lost, he would not come home until he found it. Many times he would stay out for long periods of time, and it was not uncommon for him to get home pretty late at night. Back then they did not carry flashlights like those we have today. He stated that they would just go out and guide themselves with the moonlight, landscapes, and sometimes using the stars.

During one particular week, when he was out tending to the sheep, he heard a story going around town about a "witch man" that had been seen. The town was small, so rumors would spread very quickly. People would know to stay far away from this person because he had some characteristics of a "witch doctor or witch man." Some of the townspeople claimed that some of their sheep, goats, chickens, and cows had been found dead, or had disappeared since the man had come to town. One night, while he was walking back home after tending to the sheep, he noticed that one of them was missing. It was a newborn, so he had to go back and look for it, but before he did, he wanted to make sure that the rest of the herd was inside the stable and secured, so he locked up the rest of the flock. Once they were secure he began to backtrack through the same area he had walked earlier.

It began to get dark, but it was a full moon, so he was able to see most of his path. He continued to look for the lost sheep for hours and was not able to find it. Knowing that his father would be very upset with him, he kept searching until he was extremely tired. He realized that he would not be able to find the lamb, so he began to walk back into town, thinking about what he would tell his father when he found out he had lost a sheep.

He had to walk for about a mile before being able to see the outskirts of town. As he was walking, he heard and saw a small figure of a child sitting on the side of the dirt road, crying. The child was around eight years old and was wearing old clothes, and what looked like an animal's hide on its back. He stated that the child was also wearing some necklaces made out of what appeared to be bones, but he could not make out what they were for sure. He could not make out the child's face because it was beginning to get cloudy and the night was getting darker.

When he asked the child if he was okay, the child replied, "No, I need to go into town and find my mom." The sheep tender offered to escort the child back into town,

Bess Shapiro's grave in Douglas, Arizona. *Author Photo*

to which the child replied, "Yes, but my feet hurt from walking all day. Can you carry me on your back?" The young man complied and told the child to get on his back so he could carry him into town.

As the young man was walking to town, he noticed that with almost every step he took the child was getting heavier and heavier. He politely asked the child if he was able to walk, since he was already exhausted from tending to sheep and could not carry him much longer. The child begged to be carried a little farther. As the young man kept walking, he felt the child's arms getting longer, as well as what felt like hair on them, which convinced him to walk faster, though he was too scared to say anything.

As he approached town he began to see through the cuts of the moon and the clouds to what appeared to be a long snout coming from the child he had on his back. At this point the young man began to get really scared, so he demanded that the child get off his back. It was obvious to the young man that this being was not a child. The creature's voice became hoarse and deep, and instead of a reply he heard laughter, and the being clung even tighter to the young man's back, refusing to let go. The young man began to scream and attempted to get the being off his body, but to no avail. He decided that he needed a priest and knew there was one in town, so he ran as fast as he could with the strange creature on his back, screaming and hollering the entire way. The strange being began to laugh even harder and would not get off of the man's back. Eventually the young man made it near the priest's home, and when the priest and some townspeople heard the screams they came running out to see what was going on. Once the priest saw what has happening he pulled out his Bible and began to read a few verses. At that precise moment the creature let go of the young man, jumped off his back, and ran off to the desert on four legs, howling the entire time.

During the next few days the young man fell into a deep sleep and remained unconscious. He suffered from multiple scratches on his back, as well as a deep gash on his side, presumably from when the creature was fighting to stay on his back. He could not recall what happened until a few weeks had passed. It was then that he was able to start piecing the story together and felt comfortable enough to talk about it and share it with people.

Shortly after the terrifying experience, and after the young man had regained his health, he confronted his father about the lost sheep. His father looked confused and told him that all the sheep were accounted for and safe. Some of the townspeople got together to search for the strange man that had come into their village but they were not able to find any trace of him. They did find what looked like a broken claw or animal nail on the path the young man ran when the beast was on his back.

CHAPTER 3
FORT HUACHUCA

Fort Huachuca—originally Camp Huachuca—is an army base at the foot of the Huachuca Mountains. It was the base for the Buffalo Soldiers for twenty years starting in 1913. Fort Huachuca was built to secure the border of Mexico from the Chiricahua Apaches. After the surrender of Geronimo, the fort continued due to its location. The fort was closed in 1947, but then reopened in 1951, due to the Korean War. If you show proper ID and pass a background check you can get access to the fort. It is very historic, and besides having a few ghosts, it also has a great thrift store, a couple very interesting museums, and a historic cemetery.

THE GHOST OF CHARLOTTE

The most well known and active of all the ghosts of Fort Huachuca is Charlotte, who haunts the Carleton House, the oldest building in the fort and part of what is now known as Officer's Row.

The Carleton House was originally built as Fort Huachuca's hospital in 1880. The morgue was where the downstairs bedroom is now. It was a working and running hospital for only a few years, then served as housing quarters, post headquarters, a café, a school, a vacation retreat, and as post headquarters. It is now a home reserved for high-ranking officers and their families to stay when stationed at Fort Huachuca.

The ghost of Charlotte is said to be a young woman in her late teens or early twenties. When seen, she is described as wearing a long gown with ruffles on the collar, sleeves, and hem. Some have described her as having long, flowing, straight blonde hair.

Since the building has been used for living quarters, almost every family that has resided there has had some sort of interaction with Charlotte.

One family that was in the process of moving into the house was storing some of their moving boxes in the room that used to be the old morgue. The next day they went downstairs to sort through the boxes, only to discover that someone or something had already gone through them. The contents of the boxes were strewn across the room. Some of the boxes had also been moved from where the family left them.

On another occasion, a family was in the house and the doorbell kept ringing. When one of the family members went to answer, they discovered that no one was there. This happened repeatedly. The family thought that a child from the neighboring house was playing "Ding Dong Ditch," a game played by children wanting to prank someone living in a house.*

---

* To play, one would ring the doorbell of a house and then run around the side of the house, or hide in a bush so as to not be seen. When the door was answered no one was there and the homeowners would get scared. Another version of the game is to ring the front door bell, then run to the back of the house and ring the back door bell, then run back to the front of the house and ring the front one again, and then ditch.

The family was not amused by this game and decided to catch the culprit in the act. When it happened again, they checked the front, back, and sides of the house, but could not find a soul there, so they decided it must have been Charlotte, and she has been blamed for the doorbell ringing by itself ever since.

Multiple families have also complained about the coldness of one corner of the house. At some point in its recent history this corner was dubbed "Charlotte's Corner." The corner is in the living room, which at one point is believed to have been part of the hospital's ward. No matter what is done, that one corner is always colder than the rest of the room and house.

The ghost has also tampered with objects placed in that corner. A rocking chair in Charlotte's Corner has been seen rocking back and forth by itself. A chandelier that hangs above the corner has been seen turning on and off, its lights flicker, and even the entire chandelier moves by itself. A boy living in the house at the time claimed that he even saw a dress with no body, no head, and no feet in it move about in the corner.

On a few occasions Charlotte has been seen. When seen, people mistake her for a real live human. A neighbor's child went to the house to relay a message to the family living there at the time. He banged on the door and saw a woman with blonde hair and a gown with ruffled hem, neck, and sleeves walk down the hallway, right past the door. He banged louder and louder to get the woman's attention, but to no avail.

The woman he saw did not give any notice of him. He went home a bit upset about being ignored and told his mother that the door was not answered for him. The following day his mother went to the Carleton house to relay the message herself. When the wife opened the door, the neighbor asked why she had not opened the door for her son the day before. The wife assured her neighbor that the entire family was out the day before and that no one was home.

The teenage daughter of a family that had been living in the house went out for the night and was allowed to stay out later than her curfew, on the condition that upon her return home she check in with her mother so that her mother knew she had gotten in safely.

When the daughter returned home, the house was dark, and standing in Charlotte's Corner was a person whom she thought was her mother, though because of the lack of light their identity was hard to make out—all she saw was the silhouette of a woman. She said goodnight to the figure as she walked up to her room. The following morning her mother was very upset and asked her daughter why she had not checked in with her the previous night. Her daughter explained that she had, telling her mother what time she had come home the previous night. She stated that she saw a figure in the corner whom she thought was her mother and that she said goodnight to them. Her mother responded that they had been asleep for hours at the time her daughter returned home the night before.

The Carleton House as it looks today. *Author Photo*

CHAPTER 3

Another family had a daughter who seemed to carry on conversations with Charlotte, but referred to her as Barbie. The daughter said that Barbie had long blonde hair and a long dress with ruffles. She claimed that Barbie would play with her and read her stories from her children's books.

There is another story of a chaplain and his family who resided in the house for a time. While there, their daughter grew ill. One night the chaplain and his wife were trying to get their daughter to go to sleep, in hopes that a good night's sleep would help her get well, but she was restless.

The parents went to bed hoping that their daughter would eventually drift off to sleep by herself. When morning came, they went to check up on their daughter and found she was not in her bedroom, and that her bed did not look slept in. In a panic they ran downstairs to discover her asleep, sitting in the rocking chair they had placed in Charlotte's Corner. Reluctantly they woke up their resting daughter and asked her why she was in the rocking chair. Their daughter responded, "Charlotte rocked me to sleep."

So why does Charlotte haunt the house? You will hear a different story on why she haunts the building from every person you ask. Since no one even knows the ghost's real name it makes research a bit difficult. The name Charlotte was given to her by one of the home's past residents. Many believe she was a patient when the building was a hospital and perhaps gave birth to a stillborn baby. Most of the people who have encountered the spirit believe she is there to protect the families occupying the house from harm.

No matter the reason, nor our knowledge as to what her name really is, the fact is the house, which sits at 2133 Cushing Street in Fort Huachuca, is very haunted, as almost every family who lives there has experienced.

Hangman's Warehouse

Hangman's Warehouse is a long structure made of stone in Fort Huachuca. At one end is a huge door, and along both walls are tiny windows spaced approximately eight feet apart. During the day it seems like any other old building used for storage by the fort, but at night it has an eerie presence. The one light outside the building illuminates the large warehouse door, and by the ambient light it projects you could swear you see shadows and other figures walking through the night.

When doing research for this book we ran into a sergeant who took us to Fort Huachuca's cemetery, also known as Old Post Cemetery. In the cemetery all the graves are perfectly aligned in rows, but there are two exceptions to the alignment. In the back of the cemetery there are two graves that are not aligned with the others. The sergeant who was giving us our tour explained that when the graves are set askew like that, it is because the men buried there were not buried with honor, and it was the wish of the post commander at the time that

Hangman's warehouse has an eerie
look to it. *Author Photo*

The graves of the two men set askew. *Author Photo*

they not be buried in alignment with those who had died with honor. The two graves are engraved with serial numbers 00 and 00-A.

The first American soldier to be executed during World War II was James Rowe. In 1942, James stabbed and killed another soldier over a pack of cigarettes. The story goes that Rowe had stolen a pack of cigarettes from another soldier while in their barracks. When the soldier accused Rowe of taking his cigs Rowe denied the accusation, even though a carton of cigarettes was later found in his boot. The verbal argument soon turned into a physical one. Rowe took out a knife and violently stabbed the soldier in the neck. The soldier soon died from his wounds. James Rowe was found guilty of the crime and sentenced to hang from the gallows at the Hangman's Warehouse.

Soon after the execution of Rowe, the violent killing of Hazel Lee Craig occurred. Craig was stabbed to death by her then ex-boyfriend, Staff Sgt. Jerry Sykes. Hazel was born in Honolulu, on December 15, 1915, to her Puerto Rican mother, Julia Butler, and her father, Hazel Butler. The events leading up to the stabbing are a little unclear. Many believe that Craig was married, and was believed to have had an affair with Sykes. After she ended the affair to work things out with her husband Sykes became enraged, and on June 22, 1942,

The side entrance to Hangman's
Warehouse. *Author Photo*

found Craig and stabbed her repeatedly in the neck, chest, and abdomen. After his trial Jerry Sykes was sentenced to execution, which was carried out at Hangman's Warehouse.

Stories about Hangman's Warehouse being haunted are easy to come by at the fort. Simply ask anyone who is familiar with the grounds and they will tell you how at night many people stay far away from the building.

Some claim that at night, if you listen very carefully, you can hear shrieks of terror coming from within the building, which is always locked up tight at night. Others will tell you that the ghosts of Sykes and Rowe can be heard joking and laughing from within the building. Some have claimed to smell cigarette smoke when the building is vacant, believed to be the smoke from a cigarette that Rowe smokes from the pack he took from his victim.

Many will talk about walking past the building at night and seeing what they believe to be faces staring out of the little windows. Some state that late at night you can see dark figures walking around the outside of the building. Other say that at night, if you put your ear to the door, you can hear the footsteps of ghosts walking endlessly inside the building. Most have learned to stay clear of the building at night due to the many scary tales of ghosts and apparitions being seen.

In 1877, Ed Schieffelin came to Arizona Territory in search of a mining miracle, and he found it; silver, and lots of it! A friend of Schieffelin told him that all he would find in the Wild West would be his tombstone, thus Schieffelin decided to name his claim, "The Tombstone." In 1879, the town of Tombstone was founded and named after Schieffelin's famous claim. In 1881, the population of Tombstone was 1,000; by the next year the population rose to an estimated 10,000. The county seat was in Tombstone, and it was considered the biggest town in Cochise County at the time. There were no railroads to get to and from Tombstone and the outlying areas were vast and deadly, with uncivilized men calling themselves cowboys and dreadful Apache Indians.

On October 26, 1881, the famous "Gunfight at the OK Corral" occurred. This fight was the result of a long feud between some of the cowboys and the Earp family. They disagreed on business practices, law, and politics. The Earps had come to Tombstone to find their riches in the silver mines and to uphold law and justice in town. During the fight at the OK Corral thirty shots were fired in thirty seconds. Three of the cowboys were killed: the McLaury Brothers and Billy Clanton. Morgan Earp, Virgil Earp, and Doc Holiday were injured, while Wyatt Earp walked away unharmed.

Because of Tombstone's location in the middle of the desert water was scarce, and a company came in and built a pipeline to supply the town with water. A little while later the silver mines started to flood with water. A pump was installed to pump the water out. Soon after, the pump started to fail and Tombstone quickly became a ghost town. Many of the miners headed thirty miles west to Bisbee, where mines were still active. The county seat was moved to Bisbee a few years later and Tombstone fell into ruin. It was not until the mid-1960s that a group named Historic Tombstone Adventurers came to the once booming mining town and refurbished some of the old buildings. These structures, which were no longer buildings but just wooden shells, were just a hint of what Tombstone use to be.

Today Tombstone, Arizona, gets an average of 400,000 tourists a year, most of whom grew up hearing stories and watching movies and TV shows about the Wild West town that want to see it for themselves. The town's main industry is tourism, which is apparent when walking down Allen Street. Though most of the buildings are not original, the ones that line the boardwalk today are replicas of those that stood there more than one hundred years ago.

UFO OVER TOMBSTONE

When driving through the desert, especially on the desolate highway between Tombstone and Bisbee, I always keep my eyes on the skies. My husband always laughs at me because of how intently I watch, especially at night. I simply look at him and say, "I am keeping my eyes out for UFOs."

CHAPTER 4

Maybe it is best to not search so hard for them, because chances are you are more likely to see one when you least expect it, and that is what happened to two friends of mine.

On February 5, 2012, two of my friends were in the Tombstone/Bisbee area on a much needed and deserved vacation. They enjoyed their first night at the Copper Queen Hotel in Bisbee, and were headed out the next morning to visit Tombstone. The weather was cool, mild, and calm, as it usually is in February in the southeastern corner of Arizona. They spent the morning and early afternoon at Boot Hill Cemetery and were ready to head back to Bisbee at three o'clock to be on time for dinner at the Copper Queen Hotel, to be followed by the Old Bisbee Ghost Tour.

Their car was so packed with souvenirs and snacks that they had no more backseat room, nor passenger leg room. It was really cramped and they were in a hurry to get back. The twenty-five-minute ride from Tombstone to Bisbee was on Hwy 80, which was vacant, as there is usually little traffic on the desert highway. As they were enjoying the car ride and scenery they noticed three vehicles about a half mile in front of them all indicating they were slowing down. Two of the cars pulled over, and the third had slowed down quite a bit, seeming to be going about thirty miles per hour. They wondered what was going on, as there were no obvious signs of a collision of any kind.

"What are they looking at?" one of them wondered out loud. They then noticed the occupants of the cars were getting out of their cars and looking off to the left and up into the skies. The friends decided to slow down since no one was behind them and they too looked off in the direction everyone was staring.

They pulled over about one-quarter mile behind the other vehicles and got out of the car. In the sky was a very bright white triangular-shaped object hovering in one spot. The object in the sky was not moving. The friends quickly got out their camera and took two photos of the object without a tripod, and upon review you can see that even though the frame had slightly moved, the object, in relation to the clouds, had not.

The friends watched for about five minutes as the object hovered without moving. There were no sounds of aircraft in the sky and there were no other developed areas below the object. It was clearly hovering silently over one spot in the desert. The other vehicles eventually left, leaving the two friends alone on the side of the road. They stood there wondering what the object was. They decided to get back in the car and go slowly down the road to see if the status of the object would change.

They continued about a half a mile down Hwy 80 until it looked as though they had passed the object, hoping they could see it any better from a different angle. The object looked exactly the same from their new location, and they decided to turn around and go back toward the spot where they first noticed it. They drove back to the original spot where they had stopped and the object was still silently hovering in the exact same location where it was previously. They were starting to get creeped out and decided, since there were no other vehicles on the road as far as the eye could see, that it was not a good idea to stay out there on a near-deserted road and be alone with this unidentified flying object. They decided to turn around and continue on to Bisbee. In doing so, they kept looking out the window at this object as long as they could until the mountains eventually made it impossible for them to view it any longer.

Upon review of the photos, it was very disappointing that the object appeared blurred, almost looking orb like, although to the naked eye the object was triangular and very pure white. I wonder if the white of the object is what created the orb lighting effect. When taking the pictures, the triangular shape was evident in the view finder of their camera, but the actual pictures show a glowing ball. They were sure they had a couple great pictures at the time they were snapping them.

Even though the photos do not depict the object they saw very well, my friends still swear to this day that they saw a triangular-shaped, white UFO that winter afternoon while driving from Tombstone to Bisbee.

TOMBSTONE THUNDERBIRD

In 1887, a Los Angeles newspaper wrote an article about three Mexican ranchers who spotted a flying creature—believed to be a Thunderbird—near Elizabeth Lake. A man named Horace Bell claimed he had seen this flying beast several times between 1881 and 1890; it would emerge from the lake and fly east. It is recounted in folklore tales that the devil created Elizabeth Lake to keep one of his pets in it.

In 1830, the entire lake caught on fire. Don Pedro Carrillo abandoned his homestead on the lake after the mysterious fire. He called it *La Laguna Del Diablo*, which translates to "The Devil's Lagoon." Another rancher and two of his workmen claimed to have seen the same evil creature rising out of the lake in the 1850s. Livestock were reportedly disappearing, and the ranchers felt that perhaps the Thunderbird was eating the animals. This was so frightening to them that they too left the area.

A rancher named Miquel Leonis owned a large portion of land by Elizabeth Lake. After his livestock began disappearing, he convinced himself this was the act of the Thunderbird. Leonis, unlike the other ranchers in the area, refused to be scared off. One night he camped out by the lake, waiting for the beast to emerge from the depths of the water. When it did Leonis was ready, and the stories state that he beat the animal with his rifle butt. The creature was badly hurt and dove back into the lake to recover from its injuries. Soon it fled the lake and headed east.

After 1890, the Thunderbird was never seen again by Elizabeth Lake. Perhaps that is because it indeed headed east to Tombstone, Arizona.

In the April 26, 1890, edition of the *Tombstone Epitaph*, an article appeared that claimed a winged monster that looked like a huge alligator with a long tail and a gigantic wingspan was found between Whetstone and Huachuca.

The article stated that two ranchers found the creature, which appeared as if it could not fly and was exhausted. It would take off and fly, but for only short distances. The ranchers followed the beast and shot and wounded the creature. The newspaper claims that the Thunderbird turned on the men, but due to its injuries, the ranchers easily avoided its attack attempts. At this point they shot it again and killed it. The article claims that the monster measured ninety-two feet long, and its widest diameter was fifty inches. It had two feet in front of its wings, and the wingspan measured seventy-eight feet. Its eyes were large and its skin was leather-like. They claimed the beak was eight feet long with sharp teeth.

If the ranchers really killed the Thunderbird, they were unaware that perhaps it had babies. In the 1980s, a hiker apparently found a cave. When he went into the cave to explore, he found cave drawings of a large bird on the cave entrance. After entering the cave, he found evidence of a large bird-like creature after he stumbled upon a feather measuring eighteen feet in length. The *Tombstone Epitaph* article mentioned nothing of the creature.

In 2011, in Phoenix, a gentleman claimed to have seen a large bird matching the thunderbird's description swoop down and splash in a river.

In 2012, a person claimed to have seen a baby pterodactyl under a bridge in Tucson, Arizona. It was hissing at anyone who came near it and was in an attack stance.

Did Leonis scare the creature away from its home . . . only to meet its demise in Arizona?

Illustration of what the Thunderbird could possibly look like.
Illustration by Jules LaBelle

Artist rendition of Thunderbird
Illustration by Jules LaBelle

Do not blink, or you might miss driving through this ghost town off Route 191 (see Douglas chapter about Route 666) between Tombstone and Elfrida. As you drive through the ghost town of Gleeson you will see remnants of what used to be a thriving mining town.

Turquoise was the original draw to Gleeson, and it was not long before prospectors realized that where there is turquoise there is copper, silver, and gold. The old tales of Gleeson equal those of Tombstone, with shootouts, murder, mayhem, and of course rough-and-tough cowboys. It is the abandoned remnants of a town that once was that drew my curiosity.

There are remains of the old school, where hippies traveling to Bisbee would stay, as it was sheltered and free. It is believed that some of Charles Manson's followers stayed in the old school during their travels through Arizona. Some are even convinced that Charles Manson lived in the shelter of the old school for a short while, carving his name on the wooden beam above the front door. The wooden beam has long since been stolen and we were unable to find any evidence that Charles Manson was ever there.

The jail in Gleeson, Arizona. *Author Photo*

In the midst of all the ruins of buildings is the Gleeson jail, a stucco building with a fence made from cut-down branches, presumably from local trees. In front of the jail is a metal door that has a little plaque on it stating it was the original door to the jail. It is the only building in sight that looks as if it has been cared for and loved.

If you are lucky enough to be in Gleeson on a day when Joe Bono is there, you are in for a treat. Joe purchased the Gleeson jail and is painstakingly refurbishing it. Joe used to call Gleeson home. (His parents owned the store across the street, which was also the local bar, church, and their home.) Inside the jail you will be taken back to Gleeson's heyday, with photos and antiques from when Gleeson was a thriving mining town. We were in luck, because Joe took out his ATV and decided to give us a personal tour of the ghost town, parts of which he owns.

HANGMAN'S TREE

Through the brush and over rocks we went, ending up at a gigantic oak tree known as Hangman's Tree. As you walk under the shade of this gigantic tree, it is hard not to notice a huge chain and wire cable that was once tied around the trunk, but has since been enveloped by the tree after years and years of growth. Directly across from Hangman's Tree and through a wash (which was dry when we were there) was another, smaller tree.

When Gleeson was a booming mining town, and prior to the physical jail building being built, the chain and cable were tied from one tree to the other. Prisoners were attached to the cable. Their right hands would be handcuffed to the cable so that they were able to walk the length of the cable between the two trees.

The wash offered drinking water, a latrine, and a place for the prisoners to wash up after it rained. The huge oak tree provided shade during hot summer months. Children would come to see the prisoners and throw rocks at them, since they were almost defenseless. The prisoners would attempt to throw rocks back with their left hands, usually missing the children.

When prisoners were sentenced to hang, they were taken off the cable, walked to the gigantic oak, and hanged in front of all their fellow prisoners. You can sense eerie quiet as you walk under the tree, as if the spirits of those hanged there are still watching from above. The leaves of the tree blowing in the wind sound almost like whispers, as if they are trying to beckon the innocent from beyond.

GLEESON HOSPITAL

Next on our personal tour was a stop at the old Gleeson hospital. It sat lonely, with bushes and shrubs growing all around it. Brick pillars with wooden beams connecting them were all that was left of the building. Influenza, typhoid, yellow fever, and other ailments caused the hospital to be a very busy place.

Wire cable that the prisoners were handcuffed to is still tied around Hangman's Tree. *Author Photo*

If you walk toward the road from the side of the hospital, there is a round pit in the ground made of rocks, stones, and cement that has held up surprisingly well through the years. Limbs of bodies were discarded in this pit. There was no sanitary way to dispose of body parts that had to be removed due to gangrene or irreparable trauma. The doctors would amputate the appendage and place it in the round pit. After a few days the body parts would be burned as a way of removing any disease they might carry. It was the only sensible way of disposing of them at the time.

Some investigators have felt sick to their stomachs while walking the grounds of the old hospital. Others have claimed to hear the residual, disembodied groans of the deceased. Some say that at night they can hear what sounds like nurses and doctors murmuring to each other, yet no real words can be made out.

You get a sense of dread when you approach the remnants of the building. High electromagnetic fields (EMFs) have been recorded on the hospital grounds by numerous paranormal groups. The sick and the dead left their lasting impressions on the building. Even though the building is gone, the energy from those who were patients has remained.

FOURTH OF JULY MURDERS

As our personal tour of Gleeson continued, we went to the old mine shaft, where a hawk was flying overhead and casting a gigantic shadow on the ground; for one brief moment I thought the Thunderbird legend was real (see chapter 4, Tombstone Thunderbird). The shaft was so deep I was afraid to get too close to the edge and look in. It smelled like metal and dirt mixed together, which reminded me of the smell when one drives around the Lavender Pit in Bisbee.

From the mine you can see all of Gleeson and the surrounding areas. It seems so peaceful and quiet, but perhaps it is because the trailer that was the next place we went to visit was out of view from where we were. As we descended the hill leading to the mine, in the distance was an old, rusty, single-wide trailer. It appeared to have been abandoned for many years. Some of the windows were missing, and the ground it sat on had obviously not been cared for in a long time. Dirty curtains still hung in the window and some belongings were still inside. Joe explained that true evil does exist, and the story began in that trailer.

In 1991, Gleeson was pretty much abandoned, except for a few people living in travel trailers and in old structures that offered them peace and quiet. One of the few residents of Gleeson at the time was a man named Richard Dale Stokley, who the locals referred to as "Bigfoot." He worked as a security man or bouncer for one of the bars in Tombstone and would hitchhike the sixteen miles to and from his job on a daily basis.

Stokley was also a re-enactor for the local Old West shows, one of which was performing during the Fourth of July festivities in nearby Elfrida. On the evening of July 7, after completing one of his performances, Stokley and one of his few friends, Randy Brazeal, ran into the sister of a girl Brazeal used to date. Mandy

The shell of the old Gleeson Hospital (background) and the fire pit where they burned discarded body parts (foreground). *Author Photo*

Meyers and her friend, Mary Snyder, were two thirteen-year-old girls camping during the holiday weekend festivities. Mandy knew Randy, and thought nothing was wrong or strange with him coming over to their tent to talk. The girls were later seen at Brazeal's car talking with the two men. Brazeal was behind the wheel and Stokley was in the passenger seat. It was believed the men convinced the girls to go for a drive with them after giving them alcohol, which would have influenced them against their better judgement. At one a.m. on July 8, the girls told a few friends they were going to the bathroom, but they were never seen alive again.

It is believed that Brazeal got the two girls in the back of his car and drove out to the ghost town of Gleeson. Outside of Stokley's single-wide residence Stokley raped Mandy in the backseat of the car while Brazeal raped Mary on the hood of the car, then raped Mandy again in the backseat. After the rapes Brazeal decided that the girls had to be killed or they would most likely go to the authorities regarding the crimes that had been committed against them. Stokley choked one of the girls and Brazeal the other. Stokley then took out his knife and stabbed each girl in their right eye. Stokley stomped on the lifeless body of Mandy, and Brazeal stomped on the neck of Mary to ensure she was dead. After the men determined that life had been taken from the girls, they undressed them and took them to an abandoned mine in the hills of Gleeson. The mine shaft was covered with old wooden timbers the men moved. They threw the bodies in the mine and proceeded to burn their clothes.

The men then went their separate ways after the horrific crimes they had committed. Brazeal drove his car north to Chandler, Arizona, and Stokley went to Benson. The guilt of the previous night caught up with Brazeal—the events were too much for his nineteen-year-old brain to comprehend—and he turned himself into the police. The police searched his car, where they found semen stains in the backseat and bloody pants belonging to a man. Palm prints, buttock prints, and semen stains were found on the hood of the vehicle.

He told them that Stokley was his co-conspirator in the crimes. Stokley was not hard to find, as he had earlier in the day called a friend in Elfrida to try to get a ride from a truck stop in Benson back home. The police found him at the truck stop and arrested him on the spot. When they apprehended him, they found blood on his shoes, and his pants had been cut off at the knee, as if he cut off the part with any evidence. At first Stokley denied any involvement, until the police told him that Brazeal confessed to the crimes.

Soon after, the girls' bodies were recovered from the mine shaft. After a medical examination, it was determined that both men had raped Mandy, but Mary's body was filled with mud, and therefore no DNA evidence could be collected. Prior to the DNA analysis proving his role in the crimes Brazeal entered a plea agreement, claiming that Stokley killed both girls. Brazeal was sentenced to twenty years in jail and Stokley was sentenced to death.

The court found the following facts beyond a reasonable doubt: (1) both adults engaged in sexual acts with the girls; (2) the defendants agreed to kill both girls; (3) Stokley intentionally killed Mandy; (4) Brazeal intentionally killed Mary; (5) both

Richard Dale Stokley's single-wide trailer in Gleeson, Arizona. *Author Photo*

Mary and Mandy suffered great physical pain and mental anguish during strangulation; (6) Stokley admitted choking both victims; (7) both bodies were stomped, with that of Mandy bearing the imprint of Stokley's sneaker; (8) Stokley stabbed both girls, Mandy through the right eye and Mary in the vicinity of the right eye; and (9) although alcohol was involved, Stokley had sufficient recall and understanding of the events the next day. The trial court found three statutory aggravating circumstances for both murders: (1) victim under age fifteen; (2) multiple homicides; and (3) especially heinous, cruel, or depraved.

On December 5, 2012, Brazeal was free and living in Arkansas with his new bride as Stokley lay on the table where he was to be executed by lethal injection for his crimes. His last meal consisted of porterhouse steak, french fries, fried okra, salad with blue cheese, cheddar cheese, biscuits, a banana, an apple, a peach cream soda, and a bowl of chocolate ice cream. He had no last words as the executioner pushed a lethal amount of drugs into his veins until he was pronounced dead.

The rusty old single-wide trailer with its windows broken stands out in the ghost town that is otherwise filled with old stucco buildings and remnants of foundations where buildings used to be. It is a constant reminder that some humans stand out in our memories as monsters rather than people, more cruel than those of legend and folklore.

Due to the horrendous murders in 1991, the town of Elfrida no longer holds their Fourth of July celebration.

CHAPTER 6
BISBEE

Bisbee was founded in 1880, and was named after Judge Bisbee, who was one of the financial backers of the Copper Queen Mine. Silver, gold, and copper were found in the hills now known as Bisbee. The land was so rich in minerals that Bisbee exploded in popularity during the late 1800s, with miners and immigrants seeking work coming west to find it in Bisbee. Over three million ounces of gold and eight billion pounds of copper were brought out of the its mines.

In the early 1900s, Bisbee was the largest city between the Mississippi River and San Francisco. Its population grew to more than 20,000, and it was considered the most cultured city in the Southwest. It had its rough side, too. Within the city limits there were more than one hundred bars and brothels.

Bisbee is also home to Arizona's first public library and its oldest baseball field, as well as the state's first golf course.

In 1908, a fire destroyed Main Street, but it did not destroy Bisbee's spirit; businesses and homeowners rebuilt. These rebuilt structures are what you see if you take a stroll down Main Street of this national historic landmark. In the mid-1970s, mining operations ceased, as it started to become unprofitable to continue mining. This is when all the miners left and the artists and hippies moved in, purchasing homes from anywhere between $100 to $5,000. Today Bisbee is an eclectic artist's community and tourist destination.

CLAWSON HOUSE

At the very top of Clawson Avenue sits the Clawson House. It is a bed and breakfast, but it used to be a boardinghouse for the miners in town. Spencer Clawson, who was a manager at the mine, built the mansion in 1895. He and his wife opened their doors to the miners that came to town to find work in the mines.

In the early 1900s, there was a dispute between the Copper Queen Mine and its workers, resulting in a miner's strike. While the miners were on strike, men known as scabs came in to take over their jobs. Believed to have been of Irish descent, a few of these men were staying at the Clawson House. The miners did not appreciate the scabs being in town. One night, a bunch of miners got drunk at St. Elmo's Bar, walked up the hill to the Clawson House, and violently stabbed three of the scabs to death. There is no official record of this ever happening, though if the scabs were Irish immigrants the entire ordeal would have been silenced.

Their ghosts are said to now haunt the Clawson House. When guests encounter these three spirits, they say they get an uneasy, sick feeling. Guests staying at the bed and breakfast claim to experience cold spots and unexplained noises, including pans crashing together, footsteps in the halls when no one is there, and voices heard when there are no other people in the vicinity.

Mrs. Clawson, the wife of Spencer Clawson who built the house, is also believed to haunt the historic home. There have been numerous sightings of her sitting in

her rocking chair on the front porch. Unlike the uncomfortable spirits of the three miners, the ghost of Mrs. Clawson is a benevolent spirit. She has even been known to make the employees feel at ease after they have spotted her disembodied spirit walking the hallways of the house.

Old Public Works Building

At 404 Bisbee Road, in the Warren district of Bisbee, sits the old Public Works building, which from the outside looks like any other building in Warren, though the employees claim it is haunted. The Bisbee Public Works building was the original fire station in the Warren part of town.

After the fire station was relocated, the city turned the building into the public works headquarters. It consists of eleven rooms. The old garage where they would bring the fire engines in and out is now a conference room. To the left of the conference room are two offices, to the right are cubicles, behind is a kitchen area, and behind that is a huge storage facility. The employees at the old Public Works building claim they had two ghosts that used to haunt their building, one male and one female.

Caroline, who used to work at the public works, had interactions with both ghosts. When she first started working for the public works, Caroline would feel someone looking over her shoulder. She has also claimed to see computer monitors in the building turn on and off by themselves. A toy frog one of the employees kept on her phone would disappear and reappear in different locations around the office. Once it reappeared in Caroline's desk drawer.

The scariest experience Caroline had while working at the public works involved the July 4 holiday in 2008. She was returning Fourth of July decorations to the back storage room after hours. It was dark and she was alone. After she put the decorations away, she was walking back toward the front door and heard a female voice ask her, "What are you doing? Hello?" Caroline quickly left the building, and from that point on would not return after dark by herself.

There was another employee who had just begun working at the public works and decided to stay late to get some work done. After everyone had left for the evening he locked the front door so that potential customers would not disturb him. After he locked the door, he went to use the bathroom. While in the bathroom, he heard a female voice calling out his name.

Thinking to himself how strange this was, since he knew he was in the building by himself, he quickly finished his business and walked out of the bathroom to see who was calling for him. As he did, he walked through what he described as a spider web, though we are convinced it was really ectoplasm.* After he brushed off the ectoplasm he walked around the building, only to discover he was completely alone.

Andy is the operations manager for the public works, and one of his duties includes keeping cemetery documentation up to date, as well as helping family members of those buried in Evergreen Cemetery locate their loved ones.

One day, an elderly woman came into the public works looking for her mother's grave. Andy took down all her information and went to work trying to locate where her mother was buried. Andy was having an extremely difficult time finding records on the woman's mother's grave, and while doing his research he found out that her mother had been the victim of an abusive relationship and was murdered by her husband. He killed her by cutting her throat with a broken bottle. Shortly after the passing of the mother the family moved.

As Andy attempted to look for the grave, he discovered that the only page missing from his record book was the one that would have had the mother's grave information on it. While in the conference room, looking through book after book, the unplugged fire bell rang by itself. All of the employees who were in the office came running to see what had happened to make the bell ring. Andy felt this was the woman's mother trying to give him some sort of sign. Through his hours and hours of research, Andy was still unable to find the grave site of the woman's mother's grave.

---

*Ectoplasm is a physical substance ghosts will produce as they try to manifest; when people feel or touch it they always describe it as feeling like a spider web.

Outside the old public works
building on Bisbee Road in the
Warren district of town. *Author Photo*

The Old Bisbee Ghost Tour has used the Public Works building to host two of their paranormal and ghost hunting weekend investigations. There were lots of personal experiences, such as cold spots, chills, lightheadedness, and hearing voices and footsteps. On our EVP recorder we caught footsteps in the back storage room when none of the participants were there, as well as what sounded like old-fashioned walkie-talkies talking back and forth to each other after the electrical equipment had been unplugged. Unfortunately, we were unable to figure out who the male or female ghosts were or their relationship to the old firehouse.

The old Public Works building now sits vacant, as the offices were moved to City Hall. One must wonder if the ghosts are lonely now, craving for attention.

THE OLD LYRIC THEATRE

In 1917, the Lyric Theatre was moved into the old OK Livery Stable and Feed Store to provide the residents of Bisbee a place to be entertained by stage performances and screen shows. It was owned by Lyric Amusement Company, which owned a chain of theaters in the Southern Arizona area.

In the 1930s, Arizona artist Ted DeGrazia married into the Diamos family, who at that time owned the theatre. It is said that DeGrazia made the Art Deco style reliefs on the building. Some Bisbee rumors state that one of his paintings is hidden behind many layers of paint, though there is no historical data to back it up.

Many vaudeville performers came through Bisbee and performed on the stage of the Lyric. Once "talkies" became popular, the vaudeville performers stopped coming and more and more moving pictures were shown. The theatre closed for good in the 1980s, after a showing of *Return of the Jedi*.

In 1989, it reopened as a real estate office. They closed off the theatre area and used it mostly for storage. The entrance of the theatre was refurbished and used as the realty office.

There have always been rumors of the Lyric Theatre being haunted. Employees at the realty office have told us that they experience strange noises and cold spots, and some have seen shadows walking around out of the corner of their eye. Bisbee rumors claim that in the early days of the theatre a man was shot in the balcony.

After I started the Old Bisbee Ghost Tour on Halloween, we were given permission to do a paranormal investigation of the theatre part of the building. The velvet seats were covered with a layer of dust. The wallpaper was starting to separate from the wall. The stage was still there, with the huge curtains pulled to the side. The pulley system and set backdrops were intact. The ceiling had water damage and was falling apart. To the side of the theatre there were boxes of old real estate papers. We were taken into the projection booth and old film reels were still there; you could tell the theatre had remained untouched and vacant for decades.

Our investigation yielded the existence of something from a different realm, yet we could not pinpoint who was still there or why. We experienced fluctuations

The outside of the Lyric Theatre.
Author Photo

on our EMF meters, as well as severe temperature fluctuations. Yet those could be explained by the old building being drafty. We did have a guest with us using dowsing rods have what seemed to be an entity walk through him. He started to shake uncontrollably in the seat where he was sitting. After we ran over to him and took the dowsing rods out of his hands his convulsions stopped and he was perfectly OK.

I was a little shocked when I received an e-mail from Robert Gonzales, a Bisbee native and past employee of the Lyric.

Robert worked at the Lyric Theatre in 1984. He was eighteen years old, and was hired to run the concession stand, clean up the house, and whatever else needed doing. He was paid a whopping $3.25 an hour and had his pick of some great movie posters, plus free movies! The owner at the time, Lee, told him when he was hired that he might have some strange experiences working there, but not to worry.

The strange experiences started with disembodied footsteps. He stated in his e-mail that there was always the sound of footsteps when the theatre was quiet. They came from different locations all over the movie house, but they mostly came from the second floor.

The balcony was closed to the public when he worked there, and he claimed that all the employees constantly heard loud, heavy footsteps just above them while working the concession stand. He also stated that they would hear someone coming down the stairs that led up to the balcony. The steps were very heavy, almost jaunty, the way a young person would skip down stairs. The stairs on the left were much more active than the stairs on the righthand side for unknown reasons. It became so commonplace that employees stopped looking over to see if someone was actually coming down the stairs. They thought if it was an employee or someone who wandered up there they would see them eventually. If not, it was just one of their unseen residents making his or her rounds.

On a slow night during the middle of the week Robert was sitting behind the concession stand, reading a book, and heard the door to the women's restroom in the lobby slowly creak open. He looked up from the book with goosebumps rising and saw the door slowly open and then slowly close. He never saw anyone go in and no one came out. The window in the women's restroom would never stay shut. It was opened and closed by cranking a handle, but once it was closed you could latch it down. Robert would close and latch it at the end of the evening, then do a double-check before he left and it would be open again.

Other things happened on a regular basis. Employees would sometimes catch a glimpse of someone on the balcony or in the projection booth when the house was closed and empty. For Robert, being alone upstairs in the Lyric during the day was the creepiest. The second floor was a poorly lit, dark place even at noon, and the walls were very close, the hallways narrow. He always had the sense that someone was watching him, and many times felt someone following just behind him.

The backstage area behind the screen had a similar creepy feeling, but the atmosphere was not menacing. Robert stated it was a very common occurrence to

What the inside of the Lyric looked like at the time this book was written. *Author Photo*

hear muffled conversation and laughter coming from the backstage area. One of his coworkers would always comment on how even though they were dead, at least the ghosts were still having a good time.

One night Lee and Robert were cleaning the theatre after the late show. They were picking up trash from the middle row of seats in the center of the house when they heard a deep, husky voice say, "Hey." Robert said it was very clear, in a conversational tone and a bit breathy. Needless to say, it freaked them both out. They simultaneously looked up at each other, eyes wide, and Lee said to Robert, "Yup, I heard it too, let's just get done cleaning and get out." That was the only time Robert had seen something scare Lee.

The mystery of who haunts the old theatre remains unsolved, though maybe one day we will get another opportunity to explore its grandeur and try to figure out who the ghosts are and why they haunt the old building.

MINE SURGEON'S HOUSE

At 301 Cole Avenue, in the Warren part of Bisbee, sits a beautiful two-story, six-bedroom, three-bath larger-than-life home. The home was built in 1906, and over

View of the Lyric Theatre from the stage. *Author Photo*

the years many well-to-do Bisbee residents have occupied the house, including Phelps Dodge and six different doctors. It seems some of these past owners refuse to leave.

The current owners, David and Linda Smith, signed the ownership papers for the house on Halloween in 2008, and as soon as they moved in, they noticed that they were not the only ones in the home. It appeared that they had just purchased a haunted house.

The Smiths told me that two different types of activity were occurring in their home besides the normal haunted house stuff, such as footsteps, cold spots, and strange noises. The strangest activity happened in their wine cellar. They would be on the first floor of the house and feel a cold breeze. They would check to make sure the windows were closed, and in doing so would discover that the wine cellar door had opened by itself. The dead bolt would be unlatched and the door wide open. The second paranormal occurrence would happen when David's mother would come to visit. She would sense a person behind her and feel as if someone was helping her to and from the bathroom. She also had her guest room door open for her all by itself.

The mine surgeon's house.
Author Photo

When the Smiths told me that their home was haunted, I asked them to do some research on the building and find out if anyone had passed away on site. When they got back to me a few weeks later, I was a bit surprised by what they had discovered.

In the '50s, there was a judge who was attending a party at the house. He really enjoyed his liquor and delighted in going to lavish parties with his friends. One night he was at a party in the home on Cole Avenue, had drunk too much, and tripped on the steps leading up to the front porch, where he banged his head. He was taken to the hospital but it was too late; he had passed away from his head injury. I believe it is his ghost that opens the wine cellar door, searching for a drink to enjoy in the afterlife.

The ghost that is said to help David's mother has a more tragic story. The previous owner of the house had a nurse who lived with him and helped him on a day-to-day basis. When he passed away, instead of leaving the house to his children, he wrote in his will that his nurse was to live in the home until she passed. After she died his children could then inherit the building. He set up a trust for her, and she lived out the remainder of her life in the home.

When she finally passed away, the previous owner's children were responsible for taking care of her body, since she had no family. They had her cremated, took her ashes, and threw them in the dumpster at the other end of the street. One of the neighbors saw them doing this, went into the dumpster, and removed the ashes, which now sit on the mantel in the house a few doors down from the Smiths. It was at this time that the house went up for sale and the Smiths were able to purchase it. I explained to the Smiths that I believe it is the ghost of the nurse who is helping David's mother in the afterlife; she is still doing her job.

COCHISE COUNTY JAIL

The Cochise County Jail sits off Highway 80 on Judd Drive, on the way from Bisbee to Douglas. The Cochise County Jail is a maximum security jail, where inmates usually stay while awaiting trial or have already been sentenced in the county. Usually inmates do not stay there for more than a year before getting transferred to another facility.

Jan was a nurse at the Cochise County Jail. She would take care of the inmates' medical needs, such as giving them their medication and seeing to medical emergencies. One night she was giving meds to an inmate who was awaiting trial for murder. He was in an area of the jail where there was only one person to a cell, mostly as a safety precaution. Jan went into the locked-down pod and then up to his secluded cell to give the inmate his medication. After she handed him his meds, he asked her if she had any hydrogen peroxide, to which Jan responded, "No, why?" The man responded that his cell mate needed it for the cut on his neck. Jan questioned the sanity of the inmate, but went on to finish her duties. A few moments later one of the detention officers walked up to the man's cell and started speaking to him in Spanish, which

Outside the Cochise County Jail in Bisbee, Arizona. *Author Photo*

Jan did not understand. After their conversation, Jan asked the detention officer what the conversation with the inmate was about.

The detention officer stated that they had to get out of the pod before they discussed what had happened. As they walked out of the pod together to get out of earshot of any of the inmates, the detention officer asked Jan what the inmate asked her for. Jan told him that he wanted hydrogen peroxide for his cell mate's cut on his neck. The detention officer then explained to Jan that two years prior an inmate committed suicide in that exact cell.

In May 2010, Steven Lee Townsend was arrested by Tombstone deputies as he was driving a car and leaving the parking lot of a Circle K. Townsend was driving on a suspended license, and admitted that the car he was driving did not belong to him, but to a seventeen-year-old whom he had beaten, struck in the head, and left to die in the wash near Drake Road, by the Sierra Vista Cemetery off Charleston Road (read our first book *Southern Arizona's Most Haunted* for more on haunted Charleston Road). The victim was airlifted to the hospital in Tucson, where he survived his injuries. Townsend was booked in the Cochise County Jail on May 19, 2010, on one count of attempted premeditated murder in the first degree, two counts of aggravated assault with a deadly weapon, two counts of aggravated assault, and one count of motor vehicle theft on top of his two outstanding warrants for failure to appear.

Fewer than three months after being detained, Townsend's lifeless body was found in his cell by detention staff. It appeared that Townsend committed suicide by fabricating a noose. The Bisbee medics were unable to revive him, and the Sheriff's Investigation Division ruled that it was a self-inflicted death.

Could the imaginary cell mate seen by the current inmate be that of Steven Lee Townsend? Could the Cochise County Jail be haunted by Steven Lee Townsend's spirit, who is stuck for eternity in the cell in which he took his own life? Will he torment the other inmates who are incarcerated there for years to come? Only time will tell.

CHAPTER 6

THE BISBEE MURDER HOUSE

The Cochise County Jail might be haunted, but the events that started there and led to the murder of a man on September 14, 1993, were truly horrifying. It resulted in one of the most talked about locations in Bisbee, referred to as the Bisbee Murder House (Dale Duke's house). Daring preteens and teenagers will bet each other to enter the house and take a memento from inside. There is said to be blood on the walls—both real and fake—as well as years of graffiti.

The items in the house not stolen as souvenirs as a testament to bravery by local kids have not been touched. Dust, mold, and animal droppings cover the home. The roof is caving in, and most of the windows and doors are boarded up. Two pillars on the once-epic front porch give a hint of the beauty the house used to possess, but in the following years, the elements have taken their toll on the abandoned property.

Many locals will tell scary tales of the time they snuck in and the evidence of a gory murder that took place there. It is almost a rite of passage to sneak inside and bring out a souvenir from within the horrifying walls of the Bisbee Murder House.

The terrifying story begins on July 8, 1991, in Cochise County. A gentleman named William Prince was out of his house when another man, Floyd Thornton, decided that it looked like a nice home to burglarize. Thornton had a horrible childhood and was regularly beaten by his parents. He was eventually put into foster care at the tender age of eight. He became dependent on drugs, often abusing them, which led him to a life of petty theft and murder.

Prince arrived home with his girlfriend, Henrietta Bennett, who was in a wheelchair. Prince opened the door for her, unaware that anyone was inside. As soon as Prince swung the door open Thornton shot him in the head. He took Bennett inside the home and tied her to her own wheelchair. He proceeded to continue to burglarize the home and then stole Prince's car. He drove the car to Oregon, where he drove it off the road in the early morning hours of July 21. A neighbor who lived close by heard the crash and went out to see what the commotion was. He found Thornton disoriented and took him back to his house.

The next day the gentleman went to look at the crash site. In the front seat of the car he found a sawed-off shotgun. He called the sheriff, who promptly arrested Thornton for being a convicted felon in possession of a firearm. After digging deeper, it was discovered that the car was stolen from Prince, and Thornton was arrested for first degree murder, burglary, controlling property of another, and the kidnapping of Bennett.

Thornton was taken to the Cochise County Jail to await his trial. While there, he and three other inmates planned an escape. The escape happened without flaw. On September 12, fellow inmate Francisco Javier Robinson attacked a detention officer who had gone into Robinson's cell to retrieve a mop and bucket. Robinson took the officer's keys and proceeded to unlock the cells of three other cell mates: Kenneth Drayton, Russell Keith, and Floyd Thornton. The men, who now had the

What locals refer to as the "Bisbee Murder House." There are rumors that the mine company will be demolishing this building in the near future. *Author Photo*

keys to the security doors, unlocked them and walked out of the jail into the Arizona desert. The authorities believed Thornton was the ringleader and masterminded the entire escape.

Kenneth Drayton was caught in Florida at one of his relatives' homes. Robinson and Russell were never caught, and are believed to have crossed the nearby border into Mexico. Thornton somehow got lost from his inmate friends during their trek through the desert. Two days later he found himself near the Evergreen Cemetery in Bisbee, a mere mile and a half from the Cochise County Jail. At the foot of the cemetery sat the house of the Duke family.

Dale and Mary Duke were a quiet, elderly Mormon couple who were married on August 20, 1940, and had two grown children. Their children had moved out and were living on their own. Dale had served in the US Army during World War II. The Dukes lived in a beautiful home that was a combination of Craftsman and Victorian styles just at the foot of Evergreen Cemetery.

On Tuesday, September 14, 1993, Dale and Mary left their house and drove off in their truck. Little did they know that Thornton was watching them as he hid out of sight. After they left Thornton broke into their house. He helped himself to some food in their kitchen and started to rummage through their belongings, hoping to find something of value he could use in his attempt to get into Mexico.

On his search for valuables he found Duke's shotgun. Unaware that there was an escaped fugitive in their home, the Dukes came back from their excursion, opened the front door, and just like he had done to William Prince years prior, Thornton shot Dale Duke as he walked through the threshold. His wife, who was standing behind him, witnessed the death of her husband just as Henrietta Bennett had seen the death of her boyfriend. Just like Bennett, Thornton brought Mary Duke into the house, sat her in a chair, and proceeded to tie her by her ankles and wrists. He kept her captive for five hours, chit-chatting with her as he loaded the Duke's vehicle with their stolen personal belongings.

He took their truck and proceeded down Route 80 on his way to Douglas, hoping to cross the American/Mexican border and be a free man, but he was caught by police before ever making it to Mexico.

Thornton was found guilty of the murder of Dale Duke and was taken to Florence State Prison's death row, where he awaits his fate. While incarcerated in Florence, he became pen pals with a woman named Rebecca Lynn Withem, who lived in Tacoma, Washington. Withem was a mousy, quiet, shy girl who felt that she could bring joy to an inmate's life by becoming his internet pen pal. Not long after their pen pal relationship began it started to grow into a full-fledged jail romance.

She moved from Washington state to Arizona to be closer to Thornton and eventually moved across the street from the jail where Thornton was being held. In January 1997, the two were wed in a jailhouse wedding ceremony. After their ceremony they were allowed to kiss to seal their vows and then Thornton was returned to his cell and Withem returned to her home across the street. During the next six months she would visit him in jail, and unknown to anyone else, they were plotting a prison break!

On Wednesday, July 9, 1997, a group of death row inmates, including Floyd Thornton, were working in the prison vegetable garden as Rebecca Thornton drove her car to the fence of the prison that separated her from the incarcerated men. She opened her car door and brandished a rifle, which she began shooting in the direction of the prison yard. She got out of her car, took a handgun, and started walking toward the fence.

Her husband was attempting to get to the fence as well, and as he approached it the guards started shooting bean bags and rubber pellets from their shotguns at him in an attempt to knock him down. Reports state that Thornton started screaming at his wife, "Shoot me, shoot me. It didn't work, shoot me," and thus he was shot dead, though it is uncertain whether the bullet that killed him was from his wife's gun or from one of the security guards. They managed to shoot Rebecca Thornton dead just feet away from her dead husband. Floyd Thornton is buried at the Arizona State Prison Cemetery in Florence, Arizona, and Rebecca's grave site is unknown.

UFOs over Bisbee

On June 27, 2012 (a night after a UFO sighting in the Douglas chapter), Facebook was abuzz with Bisbee residents reporting the sound of jet fighters circling overhead. I heard them too, but thought it was simply thunder from our monsoons that had begun earlier in the week. The Bisbee city manager did not know what was going on, nor did the sheriff's department. The Bisbee Airport was called and they could not provide any information because they did not know anything either. Cathe Wright sent me her observations that evening:

> ABOUT 8:45 P.M. ON TUESDAY, JUNE 26, WE [MY HUSBAND AND I] WERE IN OUR BACKYARD, ENJOYING THE LIGHTNING TO THE SOUTHEAST. WE LIVE ON BORDER ROAD. AT FIRST I THOUGHT I HEARD THUNDER RUMBLING, THEN REALIZED IT WAS JET[S], WHICH I THOUGHT WAS VERY INTERESTING, FIRST BECAUSE OF THE TIME, AND SECOND, IN THE TWELVE YEARS WE HAVE LIVED HERE, THIS IS PROBABLY THE SECOND TIME WE HAVE HEARD JETS.
>
> BORDER PATROL HELICOPTERS, TRUCKS, FOUR-WHEELERS, AND HORSES YES, AND THE LOCALS FLYING OUT OF THE MUNICIPAL AIRPORT ON SATURDAY OR SUNDAY MORNINGS, BUT VERY, VERY RARELY JETS, NOT LEAST OF WHICH AT ZERO DARK THIRTY. LOOKING UP, I SPOTTED THE LIGHTS ON THE JETS— TWO—AND THEY WERE FLYING SOUTH TOWARD MEXICO; THEN THEY LOOPED BACK AND HEADED NORTHWEST-ISH. AS THEY GOT WHAT LOOKED TO ME AS NEAR GOLD GULCH AREA, ALL OF A SUDDEN YOU COULD REALLY SEE THE AFTERBURNERS KICK IN VERY BRIGHT, AND THE SOUND DISAPPEARED AND THEY APPEARED TO BE GOING AWAY.

I GOT INVOLVED IN SKY SEARCHING. I LOVE HOW THERE IS NEARLY NO LIGHT POLLUTION, AND ON VERY DARK, MOONLESS NIGHTS I CAN REALLY PICK STUFF OUT IN THE SKY. EVEN WITH THE ALMOST HALF MOON I WAS ENJOYING THE STARS AND WISPS OF CLOUDS. THEN WE STARTED HEARING THE JETS AGAIN. THEY WERE SOON OVERHEAD AGAIN ZOOMING SOUTH, AGAIN TWO IN VERY CLOSE FORMATION.

AS I LOOKED NORTH, I BELIEVE I SAW TWO OTHERS WHERE I HAD SEEN THEM FLYING AWAY. I BELIEVE THERE WERE FOUR JETS IN TOTAL. THE TWO ABOVE ME LOOPED AROUND AGAIN AND THEY HEADED NORTH. AS I WATCHED THEM GO, WHERE I HAD LAST SEEN THE ONES CLOSER TO GOLD GULCH ALL OF A SUDDEN THERE WAS A BRIGHT, FLARE-TYPE LIGHT, THEN ANOTHER, AND AGAIN UNTIL THERE WERE SIX BRIGHT DOTS. THEY WERE LARGER THEN THE AFTERBURNERS I HAD SEEN EARLIER. THEY WERE SIMILAR TO FIREWORKS, ONLY THESE STARTED IN MID-AIR AT ABOUT FOUR FINGERS FROM THE TOP OF THE HILLS OF GOLD GULCH. I WAS A BIT FREAKED OUT AND EXCITED AT THE SAME TIME, BECAUSE I THOUGHT I WAS ABOUT TO SEE SOMETHING REALLY HAPPEN. BUT THE JETS KEPT HEADING NORTH.

DO YOU THINK THAT WAS THE END OF IT? NO! WITHIN FIFTEEN MINUTES THE JETS CAME BACK, HEADING SOUTH, AND FLEW BY AND LOOPED, HEADING NORTH. THINKING THIS WAS IT, ALL MY HUSBAND AND I SAID WAS, "WISH WE COULD HEAR WHAT THEY WERE SAYING IN THE COCKPITS!" ABOUT THAT TIME THEY LEFT US WITH ONE MORE LIGHT SHOW—AFTERBURNERS AND THEN THE FLARE-LIKE THING AGAIN—ONLY [WE] COUNTED FOUR THIS TIME. WE STOOD FOR SOME TIME WONDERING IF IT WAS OVER, OR IF THEY WOULD COME BACK, BUT IT WAS OVER. [WE] WENT IN AT ABOUT TEN P.M. AND TURNED ON THE RADIO TO SEE IF ANYTHING WAS HAPPENING, AS SOMETIMES WE CAN PICK UP "STRAY" COMMUNICATIONS, BUT THERE WAS NOTHING. I WILL BE SURE TO HAVE A CAMERA AND BINOCULARS ON HAND FROM NOW ON.

The following evening, I decided to go on my roof with my friend, Christina, to see if we could spot any of the so-called UFOs that seemed to have become a regular occurrence over the preceding days.

We went on the roof at 8:30 p.m., right before the sightings had taken place. There was a lightning storm in the distance over Mexico that entertained us with a spectacular light show. Though we did not spot any flying "flares" or any circular lights, we did see lights in the distance over Mexico that we could not explain, as well as a slow-moving light directly overhead that we thought at first was a star. Could these be UFOs or easily explained?

On August 14, in Surprise, Arizona, Kristy was out in her backyard with her dogs at approximately 11:30 p.m. She regularly looks up to see if she can spot any satellites. She looked to the West because she noticed a very bright light. She assumed it was an airplane. As she watched it, she noticed that it was at the same altitude a satellite would be. The light kept getting brighter and brighter as it moved in her direction. She noticed that there were no blinking lights typical of normal aircraft. It was just a large, bright, white light. As it got closer, it stopped moving. It turned red and then shot up into the night sky until it was no longer visible. She had never seen a satellite, nor any type of aircraft operate in this manner. Kristy checked MUFON.com and found similar stories on the same night as my sighting.

On August 15, the local Bisbee barber, Chepes, was driving from Sierra Vista to Bisbee over the mountains when he saw six or seven bright lights moving from side to side. He claimed the lights were brighter than any airplane. They would disappear and then reappear, then slowly, one by one, they turned off. A few moments later a jet started circling the area. After he made a post on Facebook regarding the strange lights he saw other people in the area started posting strangely similar stories. People were reporting strange bright lights that looked like shooting stars moving across the sky, but at a slower pace than a shooting star would. Others claimed they had seen helicopters, blimps, or airplanes, and the lights they saw looked nothing like any of those.

Some would argue that Bisbee is not all that strange, but do you know any other city that has a city council member who has a UFO landing pad in their backyard? Bisbee does! In May 2013, Peter Von Gundlach decided to publicly announce that he had built a UFO space port as a means to invite extraterrestrials to our planet by way of Bisbee.

The UFO landing base is in the backyard of Von Gunlach's home in the Warren district of Bisbee. The circular landing base has a smaller circle in its center that has Kabballah symbolism and has Hebrew letters depicted above the Kabballah ladder. Next to the space port in large letters there is a sign that states, "Bisbee Space Port." At a city council meeting on May 7, Von Gundlach stated that he built the first hosting port in the US. He stated that he was requesting a resolution that the City of Bisbee would apply the principles of basic human rights to any alien visitor.

In reality, Von Gundlach might have been trying to promote Bisbee as a place where UFO conventions could be held, much like the hugely popular ones in Roswell, New Mexico, and neighboring Scottsdale. No UFO conventions have yet taken place, and to my knowledge no UFOs have landed in Peter's backyard . . . yet.

GHOSTS AT FIRE STATION NO. 2

Every now and then you hear a rumor about a ghost in a building in Old Bisbee, though no one can give you details on who it is and why they are there. I first heard about haunted Bisbee Fire Station No. 2 in 2007, when I started doing the Old Bisbee Ghost Tour. One of the firemen had taken my tour and told me the station was haunted, yet could not give me any details regarding the haunting. I wanted to know who it was, how they died, and why they were there. The gentleman could not give me these details.

It was not until I received a phone call from a woman in Las Vegas that I took the story more seriously. She stated that her daughter's teacher had come to Bisbee, had taken the Old Bisbee Ghost Tour, and had heard that the fire station was haunted. When the new school year started, she assigned each of her students a haunted location to research. The mother's daughter was given Fire Station No. 2 in Bisbee to research. The poor girl had a very difficult time researching any ghosts of the fire station because there are no websites, newspaper articles, magazine articles, or urban legends stating it is haunted. When I spoke to the girl's mother, I told her that I had heard it was haunted years ago, and that I would do my best to help her and solve the mystery of Fire Station No. 2.

My husband and I went to Bisbee Fire Station No. 2, but the men were out on a call, so we drove down to Fire Station No. 81 on Highway 92, as there is usually someone there at all times, and one of the firemen opened the door. We asked him if he knew anything about the hauntings at the fire station in Old Bisbee, and he gave us a smirk and told us to come inside.

He confirmed that the fire station was in fact haunted, and that they had no idea who the ghost was. He told us that the firemen on duty would hear footsteps— especially walking up and down the stairs—hear bells ring, and appliances would go on and off by themselves. Yet they had no clue who the ghost was or why they were there. He told us of two firemen who had died—one committed suicide in his car and the other had a heart attack while swimming on vacation—yet he knew nothing beyond that and told us to speak to Mark Perez, who just happened to live two doors down from us.

My husband and I drove home and walked to Perez's house. He answered the door, and we were told a story of a fireman named Frank Valencia, though sometimes his friends referred to him as Pancho.

The story behind Frank's death is a very strange one. On July 20 ,1969, Frank did not show up for work. Mark's father, Cito, who was a fireman at the time and was Frank's best friend, decided to drive over to Frank's house to make sure everything was OK. Cito went to Frank's home, which was across from the Circle K, and found him dead from a gunshot wound to the chest.

The police said it was a suicide, yet the gun was on the night stand next to the body, and Frank's girlfriend was mysteriously gone. An article was written in the *Arizona Republic* on July 26, just six days after the death. It stated that a coroner's jury found that he died of a gunshot wound, but could not determine if the death was a suicide or murder. Cito testified, as did Valencia's father, that in the past someone had broken into Frank's home while he was on duty. Valencia booby-trapped his house to catch the person who had broken in, but to no avail. The gun was fingerprinted, but no paraffin test or ballistics tests were made, as they were not available to the police in such a small town. A doctor from neighboring Sierra Vista performed a post-mortem examination and questioned whether Valencia could have fired the bullet into his own chest. Cito Perez told us that Frank always said that if he ever died, he would come back and haunt the fire station.

Fire Station No. 2 in Old Bisbee. *Author Photo*

Yet the story of Frank Valencia did not match the story the fireman had told us about a fireman committing suicide in their car, nor of one who died while swimming on vacation, so it was time to dig a little deeper.

My friend, Rachel, was my next go-to person, since she had lived in Bisbee her whole life and knows a lot of the people who lived there. Rachel told me an interesting story involving her late stepfather, who happened to be a fireman and who happened to have committed suicide. Her stepfather's name was Chuck McCullouch, and he was a fireman at Old Bisbee Fire station No. 2.

He was well respected in town, yet his personal life was one he hid very well. He frequently abused his wife and abused alcohol, and was often drunk and violent. On December 21, 1988, Chuck took the family in his VW van to the Phoenix area to pick up his mother from the airport. The family got a hotel room and his mother stayed with local relatives. Chuck got very intoxicated and Rachel's mother had upset him for unknown reasons. He proceeded to throw her across the room, resulting in her breaking a few of her ribs.

Chuck took their boy and the family dog, and drove his VW van away into the night. Rachel ran down to the hotel's courtyard and began screaming for help. Other guests heard the commotion and took Rachel's mother to the hospital. While his wife was recovering at the hospital, Chuck drove out to the dessert, where he proceeded to kill himself, his son, and the family dog via carbon monoxide poisoning.

Chuck's best friend, Jim Busk, was very distraught by his friend's untimely and shocking death.

And Jim Busk leads us to our third ghost prospect.

The third possible ghost is that of James Busk. Busk was the brother of Judy Busk, better known as author J. A. Jance. He was the fire chief in Bisbee and a man of very good health. He always beat the younger firemen in local competitions. While on vacation in June 2000, he was swimming in the ocean when he suffered a heart attack and died.

So the real question here is which one of these three men haunts Old Bisbee Fire Station No. 2? If you ask the older firefighters who have been there longer, they claim it is Frank Valencia. If you ask the younger firemen, they believe it is the spirit of either Chuck or Jim. The truth is, despite paranormal investigations, EVPs, EMFs, mediums, psychics, and the like, we will never truly know. I like to believe that all three of them are watching over Fire Station No. 2, which was their home away from home.

MY NAME WAS NAT ANDERSON, MY MURDER IS STILL UNSOLVED

The following sections were written by my good friend, Patti Hecksel. She stayed the night at the Oliver House with her son. She stayed in Nat Anderson's room (see my chapter on the Oliver House in *Southern Arizona's Most Haunted*) and felt, upon leaving for home, that the spirit of Nat was with her, encouraging her to dig deeper into the mystery of his untimely death. So she did, and what she discovered was astonishing.

Not only did she become overly obsessed with Nat Anderson's death, she started to research all the deaths that occurred at the Oliver House that she was able to find documentation on. Here are her findings:

Nat Anderson was born John Nathaniel Anderson on November 28, 1881, in Claiborne, Mississippi. Nat was the third child and second son of John Nathaniel Anderson and Jane Luvinia Greer Anderson (Jennie). In all, there were nine Anderson children. Nat's father was a farmer until his death in 1894, at age forty-two.[1]

I was unable to track Nat's movements from Mississippi due to the 1890 census being destroyed by a fire in Washington, DC, and by the 1900 census, he was no longer living in the house with his mother and remaining siblings.

Through testimony from an inquest[2] into a mine explosion in Arizona, I did learn that he had been at a mine in Nevada that had a similar explosion prior to his arrival in Bisbee, Arizona. I also learned that while he had less experience with the Trojan powder used on Sacramento Hill in deep holes, he was very experienced with lighter powder, and had used that while working on railroad construction.

It appears that Nat Anderson arrived in Bisbee, Arizona, in late 1917 to early 1918.[3] He was employed by the Copper Queen Mining Company on Sacramento Hill as a powder man. An explosion occurred on January 10, 1918, in which four

BISBEE CITY FIRE HALL

Bisbee architect F. C. Hurst designed this building in 1906. Hurst had also designed the Bisbee Central School in 1905.

Designed as a combination city hall and fire station, the design was titled "City Fire Hall Building". The original ironwork above the front door displays the letters "CH" for "City Hall". The original exterior included the present bell tower, flagpole and ironwork, including the balcony, all unchanged from 1906.

The front doors were designed to accommodate horse-drawn fire engines and the first floor contained stalls for the fire horses. Vaults (walk-in safes) were placed on the northwest corners of the first and second floors, on top of each other. The concrete ceiling of the ground-floor vault is 12" thick and the walls of both vaults are 18" thick.

The second story contained a large landing for the central stairway with a skylight. A bathroom on the west wall contained a smaller skylight. The west wing contained offices for the City Attorney, Engineer, Clerk, Marshall and Street Superintendent. The Mayor`s Office was located behind the balcony, overlooking Naco Road, and contained the rope for the bell tower. The second story east wing contained sleeping areas and closets for six firemen with a fire pole in the southeast corner. Floors were tongue and groove maple.

A second fire station, titled "No. 2", was constructed in 1914 on Tombstone Canyon. This original "City Fire Hall Building" then became "Firehouse No. 1" through 1918.

In 1919 Cochise County built a Jail Annex immediately east of this building. At that time, the City Fire Hall stopped functioning as a firehouse and continued only as a city hall. In 1972, Bisbee moved their city hall offices one building east into what had been the County Jail Annex, and the Bisbee Police moved into this City Fire Hall. The ground floor then housed the Police Chief and Assistant Chief`s offices, a hearing room, darkroom and kitchen. The second floor housed magistrates` offices.

In 1991 Bisbee Police moved out of the City Fire Hall and in 1992 the City Fire Hall and the County Jail Annex were sold. In 1993 Bisbee architect Todd Bogata replaced the second-floor skylights with cupola windows and restored the front facade stone cornices. In 2009 a second remodel restored the original maple floors, stairway landing, doorways, mayor`s office, three fireman`s closets, firepole chute and ground floor. The ground-floor walk-in safe now contains a bathroom and the second-story walk-in safe contains a walk-in closet. Stained glass reclaimed from other Bisbee buildings replaced the clear glass in two of the eight stairway landing windows.

From 1906 to 1991 this building served the people of Bisbee as a City Hall, Fire

Plaque telling the history of the historic building. *Author Photo*

people died and several were injured, including Nat.[4] He was one of two powder men loading the holes in preparation for the explosion, but something happened to cause the powder to ignite without the primers having connections to electricity. The holes were not going to be exploded until the next day.

According to the extensive coroner's inquest, it was a very windy and cold day. The court and jury tried hard to get the witnesses to admit that someone was smoking or rushing the process and that the explosion was due to negligence. Not one witness testified that smoking or anything other than their normal process took place. The type of powder used (Trojan) does not explode—it burns.

There was a second powder used called Gelatine that one witness stated was used in the hole and could have been ignited by a blowing ember from a fire that was 190 feet away. Apparently the wind was quite fierce, and with workers' eyes partially shut from blowing dust, someone may not have seen an ember enter the hole. Burning embers can travel long distances depending on wind conditions. Either way, no absolute cause could be determined and the explosion was the official cause of death for all four men killed.

It is a miracle that Nat Anderson was not killed that day. He was only seven or eight feet from the hole that exploded and was blown backward and knocked unconscious. He suffered a broken nose and severe scalp wounds. The two miners that died immediately were Sidney Drakenfeld and Modesto Vastido. Two other miners, Carlos Calderon and Lorenzo Vasquez, had their eyes blown out and suffered severe burns; they died at Copper Queen hospital in the coming days. The other six injured men were Mexican laborers and recovered from their injuries, mostly burns.

Like Nat, the other powder man, J. D. McBride, was knocked out and woke up in the hospital. He was even closer to a hole than Nat was and it was even more miraculous that he survived. It was the worst accident to occur in the Warren district in some time, and the first catastrophic accident since work began on Sacramento Hill. After recovering from his injuries, Nat remained employed there until his death, no longer as a powder man, but as a roadmaster.

In the first year that Nat was a Bisbee resident, I found evidence that he was extremely generous to various fund drives. He gave twenty dollars to the Red Cross Honor Roll War Fund,[5] $200 to the Fourth Liberty Loan Bond Drive-Phelps Dodge Corporation-Copper Queen Branch,[6] and a day's pay to the War Work Subscribers in the Warren District.[7] He also registered for the draft.[8]

In February 1919, he was selected for the jury on a case: William Goar versus Frank Perley.[9] Judgment was for the plaintiff, and an appeal by the defendants went to the Supreme Court of the State of Arizona in January 1921.[10]

Just days before his death, Nat was called for jury duty on the Bisbee Deportation Case[11] and showed up for questioning. There was a rule put in place to immediately excuse from jury duty any miner employed by a company that was one of the defendants. Since I saw no further mention of his name as being accepted to the jury or questioned and then excused, I believe he was excused immediately, since he was still employed by Phelps Dodge at the Copper Queen Mining Company.

This brings us to the night that Nat was murdered at the Oliver House. What follows is a narrative based upon newspaper articles and witness testimony from the coroner's inquest.[12]

The evening of February 21, 1920, Nat attended a party at the home of Mrs. Norris Greeley in Wood Canyon.[13] It was described as a simple social affair among friends, with card playing and dancing as the principal entertainment. Shortly before 1:00 a.m., the guests left the house and walked a short distance together. When they separated, Nat escorted Miss Elizabeth King to her home on Tembey Avenue. He entered the house and talked with her for a few minutes, then left and walked to the English Kitchen on Main Street to have a light supper.

From there, he walked up to the Oliver House and started up the stairs to his room. When he reached the top of the stairs, as he was reaching to open the door of his room he saw someone that he knew, shouted, "You son of a bitch!" and was shot once in the top of the forehead; a second shot as he fell that coursed down his breast, making a flesh wound without entering his body; and a third shot was fired into his prone body in the lower portion of his back. He was first brought into his room, where he was examined by a doctor, then transferred to Copper Queen Hospital, where he died later in the day without ever regaining consciousness.

The coroner's inquest was conducted before Hon. James Allison, Coroner, ex officio, on February 24, 1920. Several witnesses testified as to what happened that night. The following is their testimony:

JACK McDONALD:

MR. McDONALD WAS NAT'S ROOMMATE AT THE OLIVER HOUSE. ALTHOUGH THEY WERE ACQUAINTED, THEY DID NOT HANG OUT SOCIALLY, AND HE DID NOT KNOW NAT'S HABITS, OTHER THAN THAT HE WAS OUT LATE REGULARLY. AROUND 3:15 A.M., JACK WAS SLEEPING LIGHTLY WHEN HE HEARD NAT YELL, "OH YOU SON OF A BITCH," IN A WAY THAT TOLD HIM HE KNEW THE PERSON. THE FIRST SHOT WAS FIRED BEFORE THE LAST WORD WAS OUT OF NAT'S MOUTH, FOLLOWED IMMEDIATELY BY THE SECOND SHOT, THEN A FEW SECONDS LATER THE FINAL SHOT WAS FIRED.

JACK DID NOT HEAR A FIGHT OR SCUFFLE BEFORE NAT YELLED. THE DOOR TO THE ROOM WAS NOT LATCHED, BUT AJAR, AND HE THOUGHT NAT WAS IN THE ACT OF OPENING THE DOOR WHEN HE WAS SHOT. WHEN HE HEARD NAT YELL, JACK JUMPED OUT OF BED AND RAN TOWARD THE DOOR WHEN THE FIRST SHOT WAS FIRED. HE PAUSED AND PUT CLOTHES ON BEFORE VENTURING OUT. HE FOUND NAT LYING ACROSS THE DOOR TO THE ROOM. WHEN JACK OPENED THE DOOR HE FOUND ANOTHER ROOMER, KAY ROSS, WAS ALREADY THERE. MR. McDONALD DID NOT SEE ANYONE RUNNING AWAY, AND EVEN WENT TO LOOK OUT THE WINDOW OF THEIR ROOM, WHICH WAS IN THE BACK OF THE HOUSE. HE WOULD NOT HAVE SEEN ANYONE LEAVE IF THEY WENT OUT THE FRONT DOOR.

CHAPTER 6

KAY ROSS:

MR. ROSS WAS THE TIMEKEEPER AT THE SAME MINE THAT NAT WORKED AT AND KNEW HIM FOR A COUPLE YEARS. HE HAD ARRIVED HOME SHORTLY BEFORE NAT AND WAS SLEEPING SOUNDLY WHEN HE WAS AWAKENED BY THE SOUND OF NAT'S VOICE. HE HEARD HIM YELL ONCE OR TWICE, THEN HEARD TWO SHOTS. HE THEN HEARD A MAN'S VOICE [NOT SURE WHETHER NAT'S OR ANOTHER MAN] SPEAK, THEN ANOTHER SHOT.

KAY WAS NOT WIDE AWAKE, BUT HAD A RECOLLECTION THAT THERE WAS FIGHTING GOING ON IN THE HALL BETWEEN TWO MEN. HE GRABBED HIS GUN, OPENED THE DOOR, AND LOOKED TO SEE WHAT WAS GOING ON. NAT WAS LYING ACROSS HIS OWN DOOR, FACE DOWN.

THE COURT ASKED FOR CLARIFICATION OF THE SEQUENCE OF WHAT KAY HEARD, AND HE TESTIFIED THAT HE HEARD TWO SHOTS FIRED BEFORE NAT SAID, "YOU SON OF A BITCH." KAY DID NOT HEAR ANY OTHER CONVERSATION, BUT ADDED THAT NAT SCREAMED AS LOUD AS HE COULD, AS IF SOMEONE IN MORTAL TERROR OF SOMETHING, BUT WHEN KAY GOT TO HIM HE DID NOT SAY ANYTHING.

MR. ROSS CALLED OTHERS OUT OF THEIR ROOMS BEFORE VENTURING OUT HIMSELF. HE SAID THAT NAT DID NOT HAVE A GUN AND HE DID NOT SEE OR HEAR ANYONE RUNNING AWAY; IN FACT, HE DID NOT HEAR A SOUND AFTER HE GOT UP. SINCE THE HALL FLOORS WERE CARPETED, THE COURT ASKED IF SOMEONE COULD RUN AWAY WITHOUT MAKING A SOUND, TO WHICH MR. ROSS ANSWERED YES.

THE JURY ASKED FOR THE LOCATION OF NAT'S ROOM [WHICH IS ON THE SECOND FLOOR AT THE TOP OF THE STAIRS, IN THE NORTHWEST CORNER OF THE BUILDING] AND WHAT HE WAS WEARING WHEN THEY FOUND HIM. KAY SAID NAT HAD ON A SUIT OF GRAY CLOTHES AND A BROWN OVERCOAT, OF WHICH THE COLLAR WAS UNDONE. KAY THEORIZED THAT NAT HAD STARTED UNDRESSING AS HE CAME UP THE STAIRS.

KAY WAS ASKED IF NAT'S SHOES WERE LACED UP, AND HE REPLIED THAT HE THOUGHT SO. NEXT HE WAS ASKED HOW FAR HIS ROOM WAS FROM NAT'S [FIFTEEN FEET] AND TO CONFIRM THAT HE WAS ROBBED THAT NIGHT. KAY'S DOOR WAS UNLOCKED, AND HE STATED THAT HE HAD NEVER LOCKED HIS DOOR SINCE MOVING IN. THE COURT THEN ASKED IF NAT WAS LYING IN SUCH A POSITION THAT A PERSON COULD HAVE GOTTEN PAST HIS BODY, THEN COME BACK TO SHOOT HIM THE THIRD TIME. MR. ROSS STATED THAT SOMEONE COULD HAVE GONE BY AND THEN SHOT NAT AT FLOOR LEVEL, ACROSS THE FLOOR FROM THE LANDING. HE WAS ASKED AGAIN TO IDENTIFY THE HAT AND CLOTHES THAT NAT WAS WEARING, WHICH HE DID.

Mr. Ross went into much more detail about the robbery from his room in the papers. Kay reported that after they had moved Nat into his room and the police arrived, he went back to his room and discovered his wallet laying on the ground near the door. He called the police to his room and reported $25 missing from his wallet. The next day, he went to the police department to report that his watch was also missing.[14] He theorized that the thief had snuck into his room and removed his belongings from his dresser, moved into the hall under a light, removed the money, then placed his wallet quietly on the floor. At first he thought it was the thief who shot Nat, but after thinking about it decided that the shooting was of a more personal nature.

The police eventually dismissed the theft from Kay Ross's room as a motive for the shooting because it was not typical for a petty thief to kill anyone to get away. They thought that perhaps the robbery was a coincidence, or done intentionally to throw the police off the trail of the killer and pin it on a common thief.[15]

DR. N. C. BLEDSOE:

DR. BLEDSOE WAS CALLED TO THE OLIVER HOUSE BY MR. DAVIS, THE PROPRIETOR, BECAUSE A MAN HAD BEEN SHOT. WHEN HE ARRIVED, DR. BLEDSOE FOUND NAT ON HIS BED, UNCONSCIOUS. HE HAD A BULLET WOUND TO THE HEAD AT ABOUT THE HAIR LINE WITH BRAIN MATTER OOZING OUT, WHICH DR. BLEDSOE BANDAGED. HE KNEW THAT THE WOUND WAS SUCH THAT NAT WOULD NOT SURVIVE. HE FOUND NO EXIT WOUND. HE THEN FOUND A BRUISED PLACE ON THE CHEST ON THE RIGHT SIDE OF THE STERNUM, COVERING ABOUT TWO INCHES. HE AT FIRST THOUGHT IT WAS A BRUISE, BUT LATER DETERMINED IT WAS DUE TO A BULLET THAT RANGED DOWN, BUT DID NOT ENTER THE SKIN. THE THIRD BULLET WAS AT THE BASE OF NAT'S LOWER BACK WITH NO EXIT WOUND, AND HE THOUGHT THE PERSON WHO FIRED IT HAD TO HAVE BEEN LEVEL WITH NAT OR DIRECTLY UNDER HIM TO SHOOT HIM AT THAT ANGLE. HE SENT NAT TO COPPER QUEEN HOSPITAL. A BULLET AND PIECE OF SHELL WERE REMOVED BY DR. HAWLEY AT THE HOSPITAL AND TURNED OVER TO MR. BARTON OF THE POLICE.

WILLIAM DOYLE:

OFFICER DOYLE WAS STANDING IN FRONT OF THE WESTERN UNION [WHICH WAS AT THE CORNER OF HOWELL AVENUE AND BREWERY GULCH], TALKING TO THE NIGHT WATCHMAN FROM THE COPPER QUEEN HOTEL. THEY HEARD TWO SHOTS FIRED AND THEN A THIRD. WILLIAM SAID IT DID NOT SOUND LOUD ENOUGH TO BE A GUN, SO THEY DISMISSED IT AND CONTINUED TO TALK.

MR. DOYLE WALKED DOWN THE STREET AND RAN INTO ANOTHER OFFICER, MR. BARTON. HE ASKED HIM IF HE HAD HEARD THE SHOTS, WHICH MR. BARTON HAD, BUT CONTINUED TO SAY THEY DID NOT SOUND LOUD ENOUGH TO BE A GUN. THEY DECIDED TO WALK UP THE STREET AND RAN

INTO ANOTHER WATCHMAN WHO HAD HEARD THE SHOTS. THE OLIVER HOUSE WAS ABLAZE WITH LIGHTS, BUT NOTHING LOOKED OUT OF THE ORDINARY, SO THEY TURNED AROUND, AND THEN THE LIGHT CAME ON CALLING FOR A POLICEMAN TO GO UP TO THE OLIVER HOUSE.

WHEN THEY GOT TO THE OLIVER HOUSE, MR. BARTON WENT IN AND OFFICER DOYLE REMAINED ON THE PORCH. AFTER MR. BARTON DID NOT COME BACK FOR A WHILE, OFFICER DOYLE DECIDED TO GO IN AND SEE WHAT WAS HAPPENING. AFTER HEADING UPSTAIRS, HE SAW NAT LAYING ON THE BED WITH THE DOCTOR TENDING HIS WOUNDS. THE DOCTOR HANDED MR. BARTON A PIECE OF THE SHELL AND THEN MR. BARTON PICKED UP THE HAT LAYING IN THE HALL AND PLACED IT ON A CHAIR IN THE ROOM.

THEY THEN LEFT THE OLIVER HOUSE, AND OFFICER DOYLE EVENTUALLY CROSSED INTO MEXICO AT NACO. HE DID NOT SEE ANY SIGNS OF A STRUGGLE ON THE BRIDGE LEADING TO THE FRONT PORCH, NOR ANY DISTURBANCE IN THE HALL OUTSIDE NAT'S ROOM. HE ONLY SAW A LITTLE BIT OF BLOOD AT THE TOP OF THE STEPS WHERE NAT'S HEAD HAD BEEN. HE ALSO ADMITTED THAT BECAUSE THE SHOTS DID NOT SOUND LIKE A GUN, HE REALLY DID NOT PAY ATTENTION TO ANY OTHER NOISES BEFORE OR AFTER THE SHOTS. HE FIGURED IF THERE WAS TROUBLE SOMEONE WOULD CALL FOR HELP, WHICH THEY DID ABOUT FIFTEEN TO TWENTY MINUTES LATER.

E. H. BARTON:
OFFICER BARTON REFERRED TO OFFICER DOYLE'S TESTIMONY THAT HE WENT INTO THE OLIVER HOUSE AND SAW NAT LAYING ON THE BED WITH DR. BLEDSOE TENDING HIM, AND THAT THEY LOOKED AROUND AND DID NOT FIND ANY CLUES AS TO WHO HAD SHOT NAT. HE ALSO STATED THAT HE WAS TALKING TO MR. THOMAS, A NIGHT WATCHMAN, WHEN THEY HEARD A FAINT SCREAM, LIKE A WOMAN'S SCREAM, THEN TWO SHOTS, FOLLOWED BY A THIRD. THEY DID NOT CONNECT THE SCREAM TO WHAT HAPPENED AT THE OLIVER HOUSE BECAUSE IT SOUNDED VERY FAR AWAY.

J. E. OMARA:
MR. OMARA HAD A ROOM ON THE FIRST FLOOR NEAR THE STAIRS. HE WAS AWAKENED BY TWO SCREAMS, VERY CLOSE, AND THEN THE SOUND OF TWO GUNSHOTS, FOLLOWED QUICKLY BY A THIRD. HE DID NOT GET UP, BUT LAY IN BED LISTENING FOR SOMEONE TO COME DOWN THE STAIRS. HE HEARD A COMMOTION UPSTAIRS AND SOMEONE TALKING, AND HIS ROOMMATE, MR. AIKEN, HAD GOTTEN UP, AND THEN TOLD MR. OMARA THAT NAT HAD BEEN SHOT.

MR. OMARA THOUGHT THE SCREAMS SOUNDED LIKE SOMEONE WAS HAVING A NIGHTMARE AND THEN SHOT THEMSELVES. NO ONE CAME DOWN THE STAIRS AND HE DID NOT GO UPSTAIRS AT ALL. THE COURT ASKED IF HE

WOULD HAVE HEARD ANYONE THAT CAME DOWN THE STAIRS AND HE REPLIED YES, BECAUSE HIS SIDE OF THE ROOM WAS BY THE DOOR. WITH THE HEAVY CARPETS HE DID ADMIT SOMEONE MIGHT HAVE BEEN ABLE TO COME DOWN WITHOUT HIM HEARING, BUT HE HAD LAIN IN HIS BED LISTENING FOR SOMEONE AND HEARD NOTHING. THE COURT ASKED IF THE SCREAM WAS A MAN OR A WOMAN, AND MR. OMARA REPLIED IT WAS A MAN'S VOICE, AND THAT HIS DOOR WAS CLOSED, BUT NOT LOCKED. HE ALSO DID NOT HEAR ANYONE EXIT FROM THE FRONT DOOR.

A. F. KINSMAN:

MR. KINSMAN ROOMED ON THE FIRST FLOOR AND STATED THAT HE WAS AWAKENED BY TWO VERY LOUD SCREAMS OF "HEY HEY," AFTER WHICH HE JUMPED INTO THE MIDDLE OF THE FLOOR AND THEN HEARD TWO GUNSHOTS, FOLLOWED SHORTLY BY A THIRD SHOT. HE HEARD NO CONVERSATION OF ANY KIND. IMMEDIATELY AFTER THE THIRD SHOT MR. KINSMAN HEARD A MAN RUNNING FROM THE FOOT OF THE STAIRS, BUT DID NOT HEAR HIM COME DOWN THE STAIRS. HE HEARD HIM RUN THE ENTIRE LENGTH OF THE HALL TO THE FRONT DOOR, BUT DID NOT HEAR HIM LEAVE.

MR. KINSMAN WAS ASKED HOW MANY STAIRWAYS THERE WERE AND WHERE THE FAMILY ROOMED. HE STATED THAT THERE WAS ONLY ONE STAIRWAY AT THE BACK OF THE HOUSE AND NAT'S ROOM WAS AT THE TOP OF THE STAIRS. THE FAMILY'S RESIDENCE WAS ACROSS THE WEST END OF THE HOUSE AND THE STAIRS COME DOWN RIGHT IN FRONT OF THEIR ROOMS. HE HEARD NO CONVERSATION AT ALL.

W. WHITE:

MR. WHITE LIVED IN THE ROOM NEXT TO KAY ROSS ON THE SECOND FLOOR. HE WAS SLEEPING RATHER LIGHTLY WHEN HE THOUGHT HE HEARD A NOISE IN HIS ROOM; HE HEARD PAPERS MOVING AROUND. HE WAS PACKED UP AND READY TO MOVE OUT, SO HE HAD A LOT OF WASTE PAPER IN THE BASKET. HE SAT UP, LOOKED AROUND, AND THE NOISE STOPPED. HE DID NOT SEE ANYONE IN THE ROOM. HE HAD LAID BACK DOWN AND DOZED OFF WHEN HE HEARD THE WORDS, "YOU SON OF A BITCH," AND THEN THREE SHOTS: TWO FIRED QUICKLY, FOLLOWED BY A THIRD SHOT. HE DID NOT HEAR ANY CRIES BEFORE THAT AND DID NOT HEAR ANYONE RUNNING AWAY—NO SOUND EXCEPT POSSIBLY NAT MOANING. SHORTLY AFTER, MR. WHITE HEARD A MAN YELL FOR PEOPLE TO COME OUT AND THAT IS WHEN HE SAW NAT LAYING ACROSS THE DOOR WITH A BULLET IN HIS HEAD. THE DOCTOR AND POLICE HAD BEEN CALLED. MR. WHITE STATED THAT HE HEARD VERY DISTINCTLY THE CURSE, THEN SAW THE FLASH OF THE REVOLVER, BUT COULD NOT SAY WHOSE VOICE HAD YELLED THE CURSE.

R. J. MOORE:
ON THE SECOND FLOOR MR. MOORE WAS IN A HEAVY SLEEP WHEN THE
SHOTS WOKE HIM UP. HE TOOK TIME TO PUT ON HIS TROUSERS BEFORE
GOING INTO THE HALL, AND WHEN HE LEFT HIS ROOM NAT WAS ALREADY
LAYING ON HIS BED. HE ALSO ONLY HEARD A GROAN AFTER THE SHOTS. HE
DID NOT HEAR ANY CONVERSATION, NO ONE RUNNING, AND DID NOT SEE
ANYONE RUNNING AWAY.

F. H. PERKINS:
MR. PERKINS ALSO HAD A ROOM ON THE SECOND FLOOR. HE HAD
NOT BEEN ASLEEP LONG WHEN A VOICE WOKE HIM THAT HE DID NOT
RECOGNIZE. HE THEN HEARD TWO QUICK SHOTS, AND WHILE SPEAKING
TO HIS ROOMMATE, HEARD A THIRD. MR. PERKINS THEN HEARD KAY ROSS
CALL FOR EVERYONE TO "COME OUT QUICK." HE SAW NAT LAYING ON THE
FLOOR. HE DID NOT HEAR ANY CONVERSATION, BUT DID THINK HE HEARD
A VOICE BEFORE THE SHOTS. HE DID NOT HEAR ANY SCREAMS OR THE
SOUND OF SOMEONE RUNNING AWAY.

RICHARD DAVIS:
MR. DAVIS AND HIS WIFE WERE THE PROPRIETORS OF THE OLIVER HOUSE
AND LIVED IN THE BOTTOM ROOMS ACROSS THE WEST END OF THE HOUSE.
MR. DAVIS WAS IN A DEEP SLEEP AND DID NOT HEAR ANY NOISE, BUT
HIS WIFE DID. WHILE HE WAS WAKING UP HE HEARD THE TWO SHOTS,
FOLLOWED BY THE THIRD, AND BY THEN HIS WIFE WAS AT THE DOOR.

MR. DAVIS PUT ON HIS OVERCOAT, WENT UPSTAIRS, AND FOUND NAT
LAYING AT THE HEAD OF THE STAIRS. WITH HELP HE AND SOME OTHER MEN
PUT NAT IN HIS ROOM AND CALLED THE DOCTOR, AMBULANCE, AND POLICE.
A JURY MEMBER ASKED HOW NAT WAS DRESSED AND MR. DAVIS REPLIED,
"TWO COATS, BUTTONED VEST, AND LACED-UP SHOES." HE DID NOT SEE
ANYONE LEAVE THE HOUSE.

MR. DAVIS STATED THAT HIS WIFE SAW A MAN GO ON THE WRONG SIDE
OF THE FRONT DOOR AND KNEW THAT HE WAS NOT FAMILIAR WITH THE
HOUSE, NOT BEING ABLE TO OPEN THE DOOR. THE DOOR OPENS ON THE
LEFT SIDE OF THE HOUSE AND HE WAS TRYING TO GET OUT ON THE RIGHT.
MRS. DAVIS DID NOT HEAR THE DOOR SLAM BECAUSE IT WAS ON A SPRING,
AND SAID A PERSON COULD GET AWAY EASILY. MR. DAVIS HEARD NO REMARKS
AND THERE WERE NO WOMEN ROOMING AT THE HOUSE. MRS. DAVIS WAS
NOT CALLED TO TESTIFY AT THE INQUEST.

The murder of Nat Anderson baffled the police and sheriff, and after every lead was followed up, still no suspect was apparent. Maybe people just were not talking, or maybe the murderer was in the Oliver House and never left. There were more roomers that did not hear anyone running away than did, and even then, only Mrs.

Davis said she saw someone trying to leave the house by the front door. Was it a roomer going for help or the murderer?

In Bisbee this was a heinous crime, even for a city that had its share of raucous behavior. It prompted night watchman C. N. Thomas and real estate dealer M. C. High to offer $50 each as a reward for any information leading to Nat's killer.[16] It was done to coax even the smallest of clues from someone to help track down who did it.

Following on the heels of that reward, the Bisbee Moose Lodge, of which Nat was a member, offered a $500 reward for information. The hope was that someone would think of some circumstance or occurrence that night that would lead to the killer. It was pointed out that a crime so atrocious could not have been committed without leaving the slightest trace.[17]

At the regular meeting of the city council, the clerk was instructed to write to the county board of supervisors and to the sheriff's office requesting that a substantial reward be offered by the county for information that would lead to the arrest and conviction of the murderer of Nat Anderson.[18] The reward was approved on April 6, 1920,[19] and was offered by Sheriff J. F. McDonald in the amount of $200. Ads for the reward from the sheriff and the Moose Lodge ran for weeks in the local paper.

I have heard a theory that Nat was stepping out with a married woman, Mrs. Elizabeth King. She was married to a miner at the Copper Queen Mine and they lived in a house on Mason Hill.[20] Mrs. King sold that house on February 2, 1920.[21] She then bought a house in Warren on February 6, 1920.[22] It must have been the result of a divorce, because she married E. B. Mathews on October 8, 1920.

The woman Nat had walked home on Temby Avenue was Miss Elizabeth King. If it was the same woman, she would have had to have been staying with friends, since she lived in Warren, and the newspapers would not have called her "Miss," since she was known as "Mrs." in other articles. It had to have been two different women.

Nat's body was sent home to Mississippi and he is buried in Anderson Cemetery in Claiborne County. His murder remains unsolved and has become part of the stories of Bisbee lore. One thing is apparent: someone did not like Nat Anderson, and that hate manifested itself in the early hours of February 22, 1920.

Murder, Mystery, and Mayhem at the Oliver House

If you have ever heard of Bisbee, or visited there, you have undoubtedly learned some of the stories of the Oliver House. In 1908, Edith Ann Oliver, wife of mining executive Henry Oliver, oversaw the construction of the twelve-room residence. When it opened in 1909, it served as a residence for mining executives and housed offices for the Arizona and Calumet mines.

There are many stories of the happenings at Oliver House, as well as several deaths. While some of them may be the result of local lore, the following are confirmed, documented deaths:

Jane Oliver
Mrs. Oliver, a widow, died on October 10, 1912. Mrs. Oliver ran the Oliver House with the assistance of Richard Davis.[23]

In an article dated March 17, 1912,[24] Mrs. Oliver won first prize for bread and cake cooked on a gas stove. This was a demonstration for Globe flour and gas and electrical appliances that was held at the Jack building by the St. John's Guild. Ninety-nine loaves of bread and forty cakes were entered in the contest, and apparently the place was filled with women eager to taste the entries and pick the winners.

Shortly before her death, a court case was postponed due to Mrs. Oliver's serious illness.[25] It involved A. E. Temby, who was charged with removing a suit of clothes on which there was a lien for room and board rent in the amount of $150.

Mrs. Oliver died of nephritis (inflammation of the kidneys). Her funeral was held at Medigovich Hall.[26] She left behind two sons in Bisbee and one in Los Angeles, California. Her son, Dick Davis, was a former member of the fire department. Richard Davis became the executor of her estate and continued to be the proprietor of the Oliver House with his wife.[27]

The Oliver House was purchased by Mr. and Mrs. Walter Douglas in July 1913, and shortly after was donated to the YWCA. It was furnished by Miss Grace Dodge at considerable expense, and the donation of the building and furnishings was made by donors who believed in the good work being done by the organization.[28]

Mrs. Oliver is buried in Evergreen Cemetery.

Constance Hoover
Little Constance died of pneumonia on November 17, 1912. She was just a month over a year old. Her funeral was held at the Oliver House and she is buried in Evergreen Cemetery.[29]

George E. Patterson
George died on December 30, 1913, in his room at the Oliver House.

According to an article on December 31, proprietor Richard Davis entered George's room to check on him and found him dead on the floor.[30] He and other friends of George had been taking care of him while he was sick for about two weeks. They had offered to take him to a hospital, but George had refused, thinking he would start getting better. The first thought was that he had died of pleurisy—a lung disease caused by pneumonia—that he had complained of prior.

George was a representative of Armour Company and had been in Bisbee for about six months after relocating from Los Angeles, California. He divided his time between Douglas and Bisbee, and had made many friends, as well as business contacts. An inquest into his death found that he died of valvular heart disease, and his body was sent home to Cleveland, Ohio, where he was born and had relatives.[31] A representative of Armour Company, Herbert H. Moore, came from El Paso, Texas, to tend to George, locate his family, and secure his trip home for burial.[32]

Nat Anderson
Nat Anderson is perhaps the most famous of the deaths at the Oliver House. In the early morning hours of February 22, 1920, he was shot outside his room at the top of the stairs after returning home from an evening out.[33] An inquest and many investigations into who killed Nat and why never turned up any leads to his killer. His death remains a cold case to this day. Nat is buried in Anderson Cemetery in Mississippi.

Arthur Lewis
Arthur died on May 22, 1930, of acute myocarditis and pericarditis (inflammation of the heart muscle). He was a miner, single, and thirty-eight years old. He is buried at Evergreen Cemetery.[34]

Among the deaths, there are some stories about things that happened at the Oliver House that actually made the local papers. Back then they wrote about anything and everything pertaining to life in the Bisbee area.

In 1910, an article talks about an unknown man who rented a room from Mrs. Oliver, but in the morning he was missing, along with the bedclothes, and the room rent was unpaid.[35]

In May 1918, Wm. Matthew McMurray, whose address was the Oliver House, was called to report for the draft mobilization for Class One in Cochise County. The men were mailed cards to report to Douglas on the afternoon of Sunday, May 26, and were compelled to stay in that city until the hour of embarkation the morning of May 27. The men were on their way to Camp Cody, New Mexico.[36]

Richard Davis, the proprietor of Oliver House, had the entire house remodeled throughout in 1914, and the paper stated that "when finished [it] will be quite an improvement to that part of the city."[37]

Perhaps one of the more amusing stories was one that appeared in the paper on May 24, 1919.[38] It is the story of Mrs. Bert Brown, late of Magdelena, New Mexico. She had been accepted into the inner circles of Bisbee society during her sojourn in the city, but was actually a thief who was found in possession of goods valued at several hundred dollars. She had stolen them from rooms in the Copper Queen Hotel, stores, and other places in Bisbee, and was hiding the goods in her room at the Oliver House.

Unbeknownst to her, a detective had been investigating and set a trap that resulted in the locating of a large amount of women's apparel and other valuables in one of the rooms of the Oliver House that Mrs. Brown occupied. The recovered items were identified by the hotel guests from whose rooms they had disappeared and restored to the owners, who expressed reluctance to file a complaint.

Mrs. Brown was given a "safe conduct" out of the city on a train headed east. She had apparently been a familiar figure around the lobby of the Copper Queen and had her meals there, but occupied a room at the Oliver House. A few months prior, her husband had been arrested by the police for driving an automobile while intoxicated. Problem is, it was not his car. He had taken it from in front of the Copper Queen and driven it into the side of the road, damaging it. After someone paid the $50 bond and Mr. Brown paid the $25 fine, he left the city and went to Phoenix.

Mrs. Brown stated that she had, "a disease born in me which I cannot conquer," and it is believed she went to St. Louis, where her father was a wealthy clothing manufacturer.

The story of Miss Hannah Johnson's wedding to Oscar Bloomquist is one of love . . . and deception. Apparently, the bride's family did not approve of Mr. Bloomquist. He was reported to be quite wealthy, with holdings in land and cattle leading to the title of "Cattle King." He was employed at Hillman's Main Street cigar store at the time of the courtship.

Unable to wait any longer to be married, the couple traveled to Nogales, but the trip took the bride out of wedding range and it was deferred. Not missing a beat, they swore the clerk of the superior court at Tombstone, the Bisbee justice who secured the license, and the minister to secrecy and were married on April 25, 1912. Both of them went back to their normal lives as if nothing had occurred: she to her parent's home, and he to work and bachelorhood.

Apparently, the separation while waiting for approval became so irksome that one night, after the couple visited the theater, they determined that the separation should end. The bride's mother received a telephone call to send the girl's trunk to the Oliver House, where Mr. and Mrs. Bloomquist would be temporarily living. It was the first intimation of the wedding to anyone and the sign of a cleverly hidden secret.

While the wedding occurred on April 25, the secret was out as of May 4, to family and friends, and it was expected that the family blessing would be forthcoming in short order.[39]

Notes

1. Ancestry.com
2. Arizona State Library Archives and Public Records
3. Bisbeeminingandminerals.com-miners list
4. *Bisbee Daily Review* 1/10/1918
5. *Bisbee Daily Review* 6/5/1918
6. *Bisbee Daily Review* 10/24/1918
7. *Bisbee Daily Review* 11/28/1918
8. *Bisbee Daily Review* 10/13/1918
9. *Tombstone Epitaph* 2/2/1919
10. *Report of Cases Argued and Determined in the Supreme Court of the State of Arizona*, Vol. 22
11. *Tombstone Epitaph* 2/15/1920
12. Arizona State Library Archives and Public Records
13. *Tombstone Epitaph* 9/29/1920

14. *Bisbee Daily Review* 2/24/1920
15. *Tombstone Epitaph* 2/29/1920
16. *Bisbee Daily Review* 2/27/1920
17. *Bisbee Daily Review* 2/28/1920
18. *Bisbee Daily Review* 3/3/1920
19. City of Bisbee Historical Records 3/2/1920
20. *Bisbee Daily Review* 10/29/1916
21. *Bisbee Daily Review* 2/1/1920
22. *Bisbee Daily Review* 2/6/1920
23. *Bisbee Daily Review* 10/11/1912
24. *Bisbee Daily Review* 3/17/1912
25. *Bisbee Daily Review* 10/10/1912
26. *Bisbee Daily Review* 10/12/1912
27. *Bisbee Daily Review* 10/24/1912
28. *Bisbee Daily Review* 7/6/1913
29. *Bisbee Daily Review* 11/29/1912
30. *Bisbee Daily Review* 12/31/1913
31. *Bisbee Daily Review* 1/1/1914
32. *Bisbee Daily Review* 1/8/1914
33. *Bisbee Daily Review* 2/21/1920
34. Death Certificate, www.deathindexes.com/arizona
35. *Tombstone Epitaph* 2/6/1910
36. *Bisbee Daily Review* 5/15/1918
37. *Bisbee Daily Review* 1/16/1914
38. *Bisbee Daily Review* 5/24/1919, 5/5/1912
39. www.deathindexes.com/arizona

SIERRA VISTA

Sierra Vista was officially incorporated in 1956, yet fifty-five years earlier is when Oliver Fry and his two oldest sons settled on 320 acres just outside Fort Huachuca. Today it is where everyone from all over Cochise County goes to make most purchases from Target, Best Buy, and Walmart. Sierra Vista has a historic McDonalds too; it was the first McDonalds drive-thru!

DAISY MAE'S STEAK HOUSE

You would not think that Daisy Mae's Steak House in Sierra Vista was anything more than a restaurant serving the best meal a cowboy could ask for. That is, unless you ask the waitresses about Charlie, their resident ghost.

The building that is now Daisy Mae's is one of the oldest in Sierra Vista. Built in the 1870s to be used as a trading post, through the years it has been home to a stagecoach stop, general store, US post office, numerous restaurants, and even a brothel.

Due to its close proximity to Fort Huachuca, it was a short walk for a soldier to make to relieve himself of his loneliness. During the building's time as a brothel is when Charlie was said to have passed away. The story as it was told to us is that he got in a fight over one of the ladies of negotiable affection and was stabbed by another patron of the establishment. He is now said to haunt the building, especially the room which they call "Charlie's Room."

My family and I ate at Daisy Mae's one hot summer evening to see for ourselves if Charlie would make his presence know to us. The restaurant was nearly empty, with a cowboy setting up his guitar by the door, waiting for patrons to arrive. There was a couple by the bar, and other than that we were alone. Upon being seated we asked our server where "Charlie's Room" was. From the front door, it is a simple turn to the right and then the left. The room was dark and a bit ominous, with booths on both sides of the walls and a walkway through the middle of the room. As we entered there was a sudden feeling of dread, as if Charlie was watching us and did not want us there. Deciding to obey his wishes, we went back to our table and asked our server about her experiences with the ghost. She recounted for us a few tales about Charlie.

One night she was working late, refilling the sugar on all the tables. While in Charlie's Room she went to pick up a sugar container when she felt a chill on the back of her neck, and then felt what she described as a spider web touch her arm (possibly ectoplasm).

She also recounts an evening when a family came in to enjoy a meal. They had their little boy with them. In the middle of the meal he started screaming and crying. When his parents asked him what was wrong he pointed to the corner of the room and said, "There is a scary man." When the rest of the family looked there was no man in the corner of the room.

Many employees feel that Charlie keeps a watchful eye over the building. A few years back there was a bad fire at Daisy Mae's that almost destroyed the building. Before the owner knew of the fire Charlie had visited him at his home in Tucson. The owner saw Charlie standing before him and then he vanished. A few minutes later he received the call that Daisy Mae's was on fire.

Charlie has seemed to make himself at home in the afterlife in Daisy Mae's. Even though he causes the staff to feel uncomfortable and a bit nervous, they seem to have accepted him as one of their own.

Daisy Mae's has since closed its doors, and at the time this book was written the building remains vacant. We wonder if Charlie is still haunting the building, if his ghost still walks the empty restaurant. Will new owners of the building accept his spirit? Will they understand who he was and why he is still there? Only time will tell.

FAIRY FIRE

A fairy is a mystical creature found all over the world. Many associate them as being humanlike, but with magical powers. Fairy folklore has many different explanations on why and who fairies are. Some claim they are born from and possess the qualities of the spirits of the dead, elementals, demoted angels, demons, humans, and even the laughs of babies.

What the outside of Daisy Mae's Steak House used to look like in Sierra Vista, Arizona. *Author Photo*

What the inside of Daisy Mae's used to look like and the dining room where Charlie has been spotted. *Author Photo*

Regardless of what they are or who they are derived from, it is clear that fairies are a popular source of mischief and fun, enticing both adults and children with their antics, and a very popular subject in folklore. It is believed that right before the solstice, the fairies come out of their fairy dimension and into ours, which is why you must be very careful when encountering them, as my parents found out.

My parents live in Hereford, Arizona, on the outskirts of Sierra Vista. Their home sits off a dirt road near the mountains. In front of their house is a cow pasture, and to the left and right are neighbors. It is a very quiet, desolate place to live if one wants to escape the hustle and bustle of the big city.

On June 15, 2012, my parents went out to dinner with their next-door neighbors. After dinner they went to the neighbors' house for coffee and cake. At approximately 8:45 p.m., my parents decided it was time to go home. They left their next-door neighbors' house and walked into their dirt street.

My mother was using her LED flashlight as their only light source because their street does not have street lights. As they were walking toward their house my mother noticed a noise in the cow pasture. She shined her flashlight in the direction of the noise, thinking it was a cow, but there were no cows. The noise kept following them as they walked. My mother started to get scared, because she could not see what was making the noise.

It was obvious that it was not a cow or other animal. It would rustle alongside them as they walked. At that point my father told her to look at the ground, and when she did the street was glowing fluorescent green. They were in a trance, hypnotized by the beautiful, glowing green street. My mother and father clutched each other and focused on getting to their house. When they approached it, their porch light was turned off, as well as the motion detector light, which was very odd. They stayed focused on getting to their house and did not follow the glowing rocks any farther once they reached their home.

The following few days were cause of much confusion in my parents' house. They did not know what they had experienced. I asked them to go outside at the same time the occurrence happened to try to recreate it. I knew from my experience as a paranormal investigator that if you can recreate a strange phenomenon then it is not paranormal.

So at 8:45 p.m. the following evening they turned off their porch light and the motion detector lights and they went to their neighbors' house with their LED flashlight. They walked down the street as they had done the night before. There was no rustling in the cow pasture and no glowing green lights. A few weeks later my husband and I went to their house to recreate the glowing green lights but were unable to do so.

We started to do some research on what they could be. I asked some of my friends who are very knowledgeable in fairy folklore. Each person told me that what my parents had experienced was called fairy fire. Fairy fire has other names such as will-o-the-wisp, pixy light, hinkypunk, hobby lantern, and foolish fire, and it usually occurs in marshes, bogs, and swamps. It is a flickering light seen by travelers on foot, who claim that the green lights cover the ground and recede as they approach them.

It is believed that the fairies are trying to hypnotize the travelers with their beautiful lights and draw them away from the safe path they are traveling on. Folklore on fairy fire has been found around the world, with each country having a variation of what it is supposed to be. In Continental Europe, the lights are believed to be the spirits of the dead, trolls, or fairies. Scandinavians believe that the magic lights mark where there is water and buried treasure. In the United Kingdom, Puca, a goblin-like creature, is said to be responsible for fairy fire, leading travelers off their path, then turning out the lights so that the traveler gets lost and has no way to find their way back.

In other parts of Britain it is caused by evil pixies merely wanting to play their little tricks on travelers to entertain themselves. In Asia, the lights are caused by a dragon-like creature who enjoys confusing local fishermen with its strange and bewildering lights. In South America, the lights are believed to be the glowing eyes of the dead that have been eaten by Boitata, an evil serpent-like creature. In Australia, reports of these lights have been recorded before western settlement of the island. The lights approach people and disappear when someone shoots a gun at them, only to reappear again and again.

Now Southern Arizona can lay claim to having its own fairy fire!

UFOs over Sierra Vista

Many believe that there is a huge underground city beneath Fort Huachuca, which is right next to Sierra Vista. Some believe that this underground city, which is accessible through one of the canyons, is home to alien life forms. This is where the government does experiments on these creatures. Others believe the government tests radar there, hence the high percentage of residents with cancer living in Sierra Vista. Others feel it is simply hogwash and people's overactive imaginations, though one friend who has lived most of his life in Sierra Vista has seen and witnessed some strange, unexplainable lights flying in Sierra Vista skies.

It was in late 1981 or early 1982, when Sean had just gotten a new dog that did not want to go out by himself at night. Sean took him out in his backyard, and while standing in the yard saw these three lights in the sky go over his head, racing at top speed to the north. He heard no engine noise nor other aircraft noises that he could make out. The night was quiet and still. He quickly took his dog back inside and turned on the Tucson news. The news was reporting that people from the Sierra Vista area were calling into the station about the lights. From where he lived he would claim to sometimes see flashing lights in one of the canyons, as well.

One day his grandmother was doing dishes and looked out the window. She said that this ball-like object was floating in the air outside. She thought they might be doing experiments with anti-gravity devices at the fort, so I asked a friend who worked there whether this was true or not. His response was, "I really can't say whether they are or are not."

Others have claimed to see strange lights hovering over parts of Sierra Vista for as long as twenty minutes without moving. Most of the sightings claim that there were no noises associated with the strange lights, and that the lights they had seen were not that of a conventional airplane or craft. Other residents have seen a row of lights blinking on and off in sequential patterns, as well as a single light that jolted out of the night sky, only to hover and then split off into two different lights. The two lights appeared to be pulsating and changing shape right before the viewers' eyes. There are also reports of people seeing two pulsating lights that suddenly merge into one.

And yet the most bizarre UFO story to come out of Sierra Vista involves the infamous Phoenix Lights. Around the same time that Arizonians were witnessing strange triangular lights in 1997, in Sierra Vista, a woman claimed to have seen the triangle formation of lights overhead, declaring that it shot out a red laser beam that projected an image in the night sky.

My friend Julian had some of the best UFO stories, which dated back to the early 1970s in Tucson, Arizona. When he was twelve years old Julian was playing outside one summer night. His childhood home was near Davis-Monthan Air Force Base, and it was not uncommon to hear and see aircraft from the base flying overhead.

While playing with his friends the sun had set and it was dark out, but since it was summertime, Julian was allowed to remain outside with his friends. As he looked up he saw a craft that glowed with an immensely bright light fly straight toward the center of Tucson. It suddenly stopped, hovering above the city, as if it was watching and observing what was going on below. Julian could see the lights on the flying craft spinning while it was stationary in the sky.

The craft started to fly forward at a slow speed toward the foothills, and as it did planes and helicopters from the Air Force base started to take off and appeared to be flying in the direction of the UFO, as if to try to catch up to it in the foothills. At that moment the craft went back to the city center at high speed, where it was just prior. The airplanes and helicopters changed direction as well and chased after it at a much slower speed than the UFO had flown. When the planes were halfway to where the UFO was, it shot straight up and into the night sky. The planes and helicopters then slowly flew back to the Air Force base.

This experience left a lifelong impression on Julian. He began to look up at the night sky more often, and on a regular basis. This was not the last close encounter he would have. When in high school, some six years after his first eyewitness account, Julian had another UFO sighting. Driving west down Broadway Boulevard, Julian was the passenger in his brother's convertible. He leaned his head back, looked at the sky and all the stars, and as he did noticed a bright spacecraft shoot at a high speed over the city. It started to fly in an erratic pattern, moving and then suddenly stopping, then moving again, then suddenly stopping again, until it stopped and shot straight up into the sky.

Thirty years after that, Julian was going through some life altering issues and decided to move to Washington state to figure out which direction he wanted his life to go. He spent an evening with his children, said his goodbyes, and drove his Ford station wagon up into the foothills in the northeast part of Tucson. He was sitting on the tailgate, watching the night sky and contemplating what life held for him, when he started to see an extremely bright orange glowing aircraft move in the sky. Just as it had eighteen years earlier, the craft appeared to fly to the center of the city and hover in the middle of the valley. Julian sat there, watching the craft, until it started to slowly move toward the foothills. At that point he got an uneasy feeling and decided to jump into his car and leave.

Julian went to Washington, and returned to Arizona in 1999, then moved to Sierra Vista, where he acquired a job with the sanitation department of the city. Prior to cell phones being as popular as they are today, he was given a pager and was on call in case of an emergency. At three a.m. one morning his pager went off. The code on the pager indicated that a sensor for a high flow alert had been activated.

He put on his clothes, got in his truck, and drove down Highway 90 in the moonless night to the waste station. He reached his destination and got out of his truck to open the locked gate, and as he did got an uneasy sensation that he was being watched. He looked up into the night sky and saw a huge triangle of lights hovering one hundred feet over the road. He walked closer to get a better look, and as he did he could tell that the light on the right was bright and then would go completely out. Then the one on the left side would get very bright and then go completely out, then the one on the bottom would get very bright and, like the others, then go completely out.

Then the one on the right got bright again, dislodged itself from the formation, and shot straight into the air. Then the one on the left got bright again, dislodged itself from the formation, and shot straight up into the air, and then the same with the bottom one. After he recovered from the shock of what he had just seen Julian went inside the gate to check on the sensor alert. To his surprise there was no high flow and everything was working as normal. Julian explained that he thought the UFO wanted to know what the power coming out of the waste station was and flew over to it, causing the sensor to go off.

He has also seen UFOs hovering near the sewer plant area while doing a fence check of the property. On the hill northeast of the plant he saw lights reminiscent of headlights—though there is no road on the hill—go up and down on opposite sides of the hill. They kept going up and down, and on the fifth time going up, when they reached the top of the hill they flew at a high rate of speed at a forty-five-degree angle in opposite directions into the night sky.

To this day Julian wants to educate himself and learn more about what the UFOs he saw are and why they are here. He feels that if we can educate ourselves, through them we might be able to learn their technology and in return be able to live in a world where we will not be destroying our planet the way we currently do.

CHAPTER 8

TUCSON

Some 12,000 years ago, the first Paleo-Indians roamed what is now Tucson. Evidence of such tribes has been found along the Santa Cruz River. In 1692, the Mission San Xavier del Bac was founded along the Santa Cruz River, and this settlement was named Tucson. In March 1856, the United States captured Tucson from Mexico. It had been a part of Mexico until the point of the Gadsden Purchase. In 1885, after Tucson became the capital of the Confederate Arizona Territory, and after Arizona became part of the New Mexico Territory, the University of Arizona was founded in the city.

After World War I, many veterans who were gassed during the war started coming to Tucson because of the dry air that was good for their lungs. Tucson then started development of the veteran's hospital. Since then people have come from all over the world to Tucson due to the clean, dry air and warm climate.

In the 1880s, the city of Tucson received a very special gift: the Southern Pacific Railroad. In that year the population of Tucson grew to 8,000. The railroad is what kept the city alive and thriving, because it was now connected to the rest of the world. It brought people heading west to California's gold rush. Some of these people stopped in Tucson, seeking to find wealth there. In 1912, Arizona became a state.

Today Tucson's second-biggest employer is the University of Arizona; Davis-Monthan Air Force Base also provides the city with lots of job opportunities. Tourism is another huge industry in Tucson, with an estimated 3.5 million visitors each year.

EL TIRODITO WISHING SHRINE

Not far from the hustle and bustle of downtown Tucson sits the Wishing Shrine, more commonly known among locals as El Tirodito. As you approach the shrine, it is not uncommon to see wax remains of candles, notes and letters stuck in cracks, trinkets given as offerings, and flowers as well as toys, coins, and other objects people have left as an offering to the Wishing Shrine.

El Tirodito, which translates to "The Castaway," is the only shrine on the National Register of Historical Places dedicated to a sinner instead of a saint.

There are a few conflicting stories behind El Tirodito and all are tragic.

The first story involves a love triangle and the death of an adulteress. A married woman was madly in love with a man other than her husband and the two started a love affair. When her husband found out about his wife's love for another man he became infuriated and shot the man, murdering his wife's lover in cold blood. The lover had died a sinner, and therefore could not be buried in the consecrated cemetery. Many believe the shrine was built in the early 1870s on the exact location where the lover died. Locals would light candles on his death site and pray in hopes that his soul would be saved and taken to heaven.

The second story involves a gentleman who every day would watch a woman from afar. As the days, weeks, months, and years went on he fell more and more in love with her. Being a shy man, he never approached her or even tried to talk to her.

The El Tiradito shrine
in Tucson, Arizona.
Author Photo

One day he decided that he was going to talk to her parents and ask for her hand, only to find out that she had been promised to another man. His heart had been broken, and he felt it would be impossible to heal. He then took a gun and ended his life. Since he committed suicide he was considered a sinner and could not be buried in a Catholic cemetery. He was buried on the spot where he killed himself and the shrine was then erected. His friends and family built the shrine and would light candles in hopes that his soul would be returned to heaven.

The third story involving the origin of El Tiradito is that of a father and son who had never met before. A mother, on her deathbed in Mexico, sent her son to find his father in Tucson, as it was her dying wish that they meet each other before her passing. The son traveled to Tucson and went door to door searching for his father. When he found his father's home, a beautiful young woman answered the door, and he quickly found out that his father had taken himself a new bride.

The son explained who he was and why he was there. The young woman told the young man to come inside and rest until her husband got home. When the husband arrived back from his work he found his wife and a young man whom he did not know alone together in his house. He became outraged, and before either of them had time to explain what was happening, the father had taken an ax from his bundle, chased his son outside into the street, and killed him.

The Wishing Shrine currently sits at 356 South Main Street, as it was moved from its original location in 1928 to Simpson and Main, and then later moved again to its current location. In 1988, it was put on the National Register of Historic Places in hopes of saving its neighborhood from an expressway the city was planning to put there.

The Wishing Shrine plays a huge role in Latino culture and folklore. Many believe if you light a candle while making a wish and the candle is still lit the next day, your wish is sure to come true. Others write notes on pieces of paper and stick them in the cracks of the structure, hoping that their prayers will be answered. The most common prayer or wish asked for is the mending of a broken heart.

LA LLORONA

When we first started doing the Old Bisbee Ghost Tour, I had guests on almost every tour ask me if I had heard about the local ghost known as La Llorona. Not originally from Arizona, I had to research this ghost that was said to haunt Bisbee and Douglas. I soon discovered that La Llorona was a story that was told all over the American Southwest, as well as Mexico.

El Tiradito Shrine in Tucson. *Author Photo*

CHAPTER 8

There are some ghost stories that have been around for so long that people can't remember their origin. Most are cautionary tales; folklore stories told to warn the hearer of danger or to teach them a lesson.

The story of La Llorona is this type of ghost story. The story's origins are unknown, yet many believe it began in Mexico, as it is a very popular story in Latino cultures from Mexico to the American Southwest. The urban legend says that La Llorona is a tall, thin, attractive woman with long, dark, flowing hair that is usually seen wearing a long flowing gown. She tends to haunt areas near bodies of water, creeks, and rivers. She will go up to houses and peer in the windows. If she spots misbehaving children while looking through their windows, she will kidnap them and take them to the water, where she promptly drowns them. It is also believed that if children are out by themselves after dark La Llorona will find them and snatch them up.

The most popular story of La Llorona is of a single beautiful woman named Maria who had a couple children from a previous relationship. The father of her children had left her and she became a single mother. She was very poor, but very beautiful. Trying to use her beauty as an advantage, Maria would leave her children to go out at night and flirt with the wealthy men traveling through her town.

One version of the story says that Maria fell madly in love with a wealthy man who did not like her children and did not want a woman who had children from previous relationships, so she took her children to the local river and drowned them. When she returned to be with her man, he could not believe what she had done and told her that he wanted nothing to do with her. She was so devastated by his rejection that she went back to the river where she had murdered her children and drowned herself.

Another version of the story states that Maria would neglect her children and leave them alone to wander by themselves near a riverbank while she entertained her gentleman callers. One night they accidentally fell while playing too close to the river and drowned in the rushing water. When morning came and Maria was trying to find her children, she found their lifeless bodies on the edge of the river.

In despair over what she had done she stopped eating. She would walk the banks of the river day and night, crying and screaming while searching for her children, so emotionally distraught that she would forget they were dead. Eventually Maria withered away to mere skin and bones, and then died on the banks of the river where her children had died.

In all versions of the story, when Maria got to the gates of heaven, she was refused entry due to the sins she had committed against her children and herself. She was told that the only way she could get into heaven was if she went back to Earth to find the souls of her dead children. So she wanders Earth weeping, searching for the souls of her children, hence the name La Llorona, which means "Weeping Woman" in Spanish. The story goes that sometimes she gets so desperate to find her children that she will kidnap other people's children in hopes that they will pass for her own. She is also known to take children who have disobeyed their parents.

The story of La Llorona has been told in Latino cultures from generation to generation, usually told by parents to their children in hopes that the story will scare them into behaving and not sneaking around the water's edge or venturing out by themselves after dark.

GHOST OF ST. JOSEPH'S HOSPITAL

Few would think that a hospital would be haunted. Usually it is a sterile environment where people go to improve their health. But what happens to the souls of the people who die there? Perhaps their souls remain, which is why hospital hauntings are not as uncommon as one would think. It is believed that in most running hospitals, the nurses and doctors are too busy trying to keep their patients alive and they do not pay attention to the spirits of the deceased that still roam the halls.

Sammy Hedwig might have been one of those nurses, working too hard to take notice, or perhaps it was the spirit that kept her working so hard . . .

Sammy worked on the second floor of St Joseph's Hospital. It was about 11 p.m., and the thirty-six patients she was looking after were all resting peacefully in their rooms. She was seated at the nurses' station when she heard a man's voice call, "Nurse, nurse." She got up and went to the first room of the hallway. He yelled again and she knew she was at the right place; the man's bed was on the far side of the room, next to the window.

There was another patient in the room in the first bed, but he had been non-responsive for the last two days and was an active hospice case in the unit. She approached the yelling man, who was about forty-five years old and recovering from minor knee surgery. The patient said, "Man, there is something under that bed over there." Sammy turned on his light and showed him there was nothing there; the other patient appeared to be resting comfortably. She told him that she would look up any medications he was on, because he seemed to be having hallucinations. She went to the med book and saw he had only had Tylenol four hours before.

Before Sammy could get back to the nurses' station the man began yelling again. She went into his room, only to find him in a panic, and he said, "Someone came out from under that bed and was pulling on the guy's feet!" Sammy turned and looked at the comatose patient in the first bed, only to discover his feet were hanging over the end of the raised footboard.

There was no way this patient could have done this himself because he had not moved in days. At this point Sammy was scared, but trying her best to stay professional, she told the other patient he was having weird dreams because of the stress of his surgery. She called for help, and when the second nurse arrived they pulled the hospice patient up in bed and got his feet all tucked in. The other patient appeared to have calmed down, so they left the room and headed back to the nurses' station.

As soon as they approached the nurses' station the patient started screaming again. As Sammy entered his room the patient claimed that he thought he saw someone, and again the other patient's feet were uncovered and hanging over the footboard. After settling the panicked patient and covering the other man's feet again she left the room.

A few minutes later the patient started to scream that he was leaving the hospital because some weird stuff was happening. He said, "A man came out from under that bed! He came over to me and said, 'If you call her again, you're next!'" There was definitely a feeling of dread and darkness in the room. The patient described the creature as having no face, and it was wearing a hat and a long coat or cloak. This poor man was scared for his life and hopped on one leg out the door of the recovery room. His wife came to pick him up not more than an hour later after he refused to step foot in the recovery room again. After he left, the two nurses settled the hospice patient back into bed with his feet covered.

Sammy went to check on the patient that remained in the room a short while later. She looked at him in total disbelief; after pulling him up in bed and covering his feet three times in an hour his feet were sticking up, uncovered over the footboard again, except this time it was obvious that he was dead. Due to frequent deaths in the room, after this incident it was blessed and turned into an exam room for the next five years. In recent years it has since been turned back into a patient recovery room, though the question on everyone's mind is whom will this dark shadow figure visit and who will be next on its list?

In 2010, after having such crazy spirt encounters, Sammy became pretty clinical about any experiences and easily brushed them off. In Fall 2010, Sammy, a friend, and a coworker decided to have some fun with a "ghost radar" app on their phone (mind you, I personally do not believe such apps work for detecting ghosts and are just fun to use to scare your friends). They decided to go to the morgue and test it out. When they went inside they found the room empty, and the phone app started blinking with red dots; at this point they looked at each other and laughed. Not a moment later the toilet in the morgue restroom flushed. You could have heard a pin drop after that!

Sammy went to check it out, only to find an old toilet that in no way could have an auto flush. After a few moments she said out loud, "Well, if you're here what's your name?" and immediately after that the ghost radar said, "Harry." The three of them went to look at the death log kept in the morgue and they discovered that a man named Harold was just removed from the morgue fifteen minutes earlier and his nickname was Harry.

Was the ghost radar phone app really detecting the spirit of a deceased man in the morgue of the hospital? Or was it simply a coincidence?

Her personal stories do not end there. Her husband was a young child when his grandfather passed away in Tucson Estates, out by Old Tucson Studios, in 1978. The night he passed away her husband woke up and saw him sitting in a metal folding chair across from the head of his bed. The grandfather had a blue glow around him and began to talk to the boy, and told him not to be afraid. They continued to talk, but her husband can no longer remember what they said to one another. The next day her husband's aunt took his picture in that same chair and the yellow shirt he was wearing turned that same color blue when the pictures were developed.

In their current home, her husband and twenty-four-year-old daughter have seen a ghost cat, described as a large grey tabby cat. They mostly see this ghostly feline on the stairs and walking in the hallway toward her daughter's room. At first they thought he must have tagged along with their daughter from Rota, Spain, where she was stationed for a while.

Her daughter stated that there were many feral cats, and they would often meet their demise in the road in front of her house. After she moved into her own place they still continued to see the cat at their current home, so Sammy began to think its spirit was attached to the house and did not follow her daughter home from Spain. They spotted him now and then, but when their daughter moved back in a year later, the ghost cat became very active and they saw him frequently over the course of a few days.

Shortly after she moved back in their daughter discovered signs in their guest room of possible entrapment of an animal. The door was heavily scratched, and more disturbing was the back of the closet door, where it appeared a cat may have been trapped inside for a long period of time. Evidence of cats attempting to scratch their way out of the closet were present. They all felt awful that this was most likely ghost cat's fate in the closet, abandoned by a renter long ago. The entire family felt heartbroken and offered a prayer, silently stating that they were sorry this had happened. After the prayer was given they each saw the ghost cat once more and then it never made an appearance again. Hopefully it is frolicking in a mice field in the sky.

CINEWORLD 4 THEATRE

The Cineworld 4 Theatre sits alone in a shopping center on Speedway Boulevard in Tucson, Arizona. The building cost $350,000 to build in 1971, and was built in the mid-century modern architectural style by Ann Rysdale. Rysdale was famous for being the only licensed female architect from the 1940s through the 1960s in Arizona.

The venue consisted of four theatres, each seating 250 people. It was originally owned by Cineworld Corporation of California, then TM Theatres bought it and then sold it to AMC Theatres. Now it sits vacant in the far corner of a parking lot, unused and untouched. After the moviegoers left, it became the home of a Chuck E. Cheese in 2009, which five years later moved out and relocated across the street. Could it have been the ghost that forced the fun family venue to move?

In June 1994, Brandyn Enfield was twenty years old and got a job at a movie theatre in Tucson—Cineworld 4 Theatres—where she had seen movies her entire life. She once had the experience as a patron of having her shirt tugged from behind while waiting in line for snacks. She spun around and could not identify who had

What the outside of the Cineworld 4 Theatre looked like at the time this book was published. *Author Photo*

done it, but since the lobby was full of other people, she assumed that it was one of the other customers and dismissed it. This was simply a foreshadowing of what was to happen years later.

It was her second week working at the theatre, and the last showing of the movies had all started, so Brandyn began cleaning up the concession stand as part of her normal duties.

The one other person working concessions that night was in the kitchen doing dishes as Brandyn began to clean the popcorn popper. All of a sudden she felt her ponytail being pulled—not hard enough to hurt, but hard enough to jerk her head back a bit. She assumed it was the doorman that night teasing and flirting with her and told him out loud to "cut it out" while continuing her work. About thirty seconds later her hair was pulled again a little harder. This time Brandyn immediately turned around and said rather loudly, "Stop it!" only to see that the doorman was on the other side of the concession counter and across the lobby, looking startled by her outburst.

According to Brandyn, there was no way he could have jumped the counter and run the thirty feet to where he was in the second it took her to turn around. He asked what happened and when she told him, he laughed and said it was just the ghost, as though she should have known. Her coworker in the kitchen popped out of the door, arms covered in suds, and asked what was going on. The doorman told her the ghost had introduced himself to Brandyn. Brandyn was not sure whether she should believe them. They could have been trying to haze the new girl, so she asked what kind of other things had happened around there that caused them to believe the theatre was haunted. They then began to tell Brandyn that things would go missing from where they had been put, only to appear in another place later. Footsteps were heard on the stairs leading to the projection booth when no one was there. On more than one occasion, people had seen a mop moving by itself in the janitor's closet. The big story was that one of the doormen had seen a man sitting in one of the theatres after hours, but when he approached the man, the figure disappeared into thin air. They searched the building for him but never found anyone.

A month went by before the ghost showed off for Brandyn again. During that time she had been trained to operate the film projectors, and one night she was working as both doorman and projectionist. She would tear tickets until it was time to start the movie, then the manager would take over at the door and Brandyn would unlock the door to the projection room and go upstairs to rethread the film through the projector, press the button to start the movie at the right time, then come back down and resume tearing tickets.

It was about halfway through her shift and one of the movies had ended. She knew it was time to rethread the projector for the next showing and unlocked the door to the stairwell leading to the booth. She went up the stairs to the projection room, only to find the film already threaded through the machine. She approached it cautiously, as she had the only key to the locked booth in her pocket and could not figure out who could have unlocked the door to the projection booth, gone up the stairs, and rethreaded the movie without anyone noticing. The previous showing had just ended a few minutes before and all of the film should have still been on the platter.

When she got closer, she watched the little hinged gate that secures the film in front of the projection light swing closed by itself and click into place, finishing the job for her. She felt the hair on the back of her neck stand up and froze. It was surreal to see something move by itself, and it took her a moment to process what had just happened. Finally believing that the stories of the ghost were true Brandyn said, "Thank you" aloud and frantically ran down the stairs. She gave the manager the key and asked him to start the rest of the movies that night. He seemed amused and asked if it was the ghost again, to which Brandyn confirmed his question with a head nod, indicating yes, it was the ghost. After that incident the ghost rarely made itself known to Brandyn, for she only had a couple small experiences after that night: a hand on her shoulder while sitting in the back row watching a movie, and hearing the door to the booth slam and ghostly footsteps with no one there.

A few months later the theatre was closed down and remodeled into a Chuck E. Cheese. Before the Chuck E. Cheese moved across the street to its current location parents would take their children there, unaware that the place was haunted. People

The inside of the old Cineworld 4 Theatre at the time this book was published. *Author Photo*

would claim that there was a heavy, sad feeling in the building. Some said that the animatronics would move by themselves when there was not a show being performed, and others state that they had the constant feeling of always being watched when inside.

Brandyn always wondered if the ghost was still there and got her answer in 1997, when she was working at a sandwich shop in the same neighborhood. One slow afternoon the employees were bored and began telling ghost stories. The new kid told them that at his last job the mop would move by itself in the janitor's closet. Brandyn asked him where he used to work, and he told her it was the Chuck E. Cheese. She was glad to hear that the ghost was still up to its old antics even after the building changed from a theatre to a Chuck E. Cheese.

RITA RANCH

Fifteen miles south of Tucson lies a housing development right out of the opening of the TV show *Weeds*. The homes are all lined up perfectly, their lawns are mowed, and if they do not have lawns then they have flawless rock gardens with cacti planted in a perfect Fung Shui arrangement.

Parents walk their children to the local elementary school, which is only a few blocks away, with little worry. Children ride their bikes in the streets before their parents return home from work with a complete sense of safety. What few in this neighborhood realize is that more than one hundred years ago, this homage to suburbia life was the site of an extreme and deadly train wreck.

On January 28, 1903, John Bruce, a thirty-year veteran responsible for bringing the first train to Tucson in 1880, conducted the Pacific Coast Express train. Bruce had stopped the train at Vail Station, one of many stops on its way to take the train's passengers to San Francisco. It was already running more than two hours late, but they were told to pick up orders in Vail, so they did. The first order told them to stop at the Wilmot station to pick up freight. The second order was to meet the Crescent City Express, which was headed in the opposite, eastbound direction, at Esmond. The conductor never received his second order instructing him to pull over to the Esmond siding to allow the Crescent City Express to pass safely.

At the same time, the Crescent City Express, being conducted by Bob Wilkey, was also running late as it was heading eastbound on its way to drop off its passengers in New Orleans. The Crescent City Express, unaware that the Pacific Coast Express did not receive the message, was riding along the tracks at seventy miles per hour, trying to make up some lost time.

The trains hit head on at what is now the corner of Rita Road and Houghton Road, causing an immense eruption of fire fueled by the oil that both trains ran on. The fire from the crash caused such huge flames that they could be seen from Tucson proper.

One report stated that the impact was so intense it caused the last car on one of the trains to roll downhill for miles. Though no record exists of how many passengers were on each train, it is believed that fourteen people were killed in the crash, including both conductors. Most of the bodies were identified through personal artifacts, such as jewelry, as the bodies were burned so badly it was impossible to identify them any other way.

Today there stands a plaque honoring the crash and its victims at the corner where it occurred, but the story does not end there. It appears the ghosts of the wreck's victims haunt the quiet neighborhood of Rita Ranch. The housing development began being built in the 1990s. One of my friends lives at the corner of Rita Road and Esmond Loop. Her house was built in 1998, but she did not move in until 2011. After moving in, she started having paranormal experiences in her home, as well as in her yard. She has seen the spirits of two gentlemen wearing what appears to be late-Victorian-era-style clothing.

The ghost sightings are so commonplace in their home that Ivy and her husband Jeff have accepted them as part of their daily life.

One evening, while enjoying quiet time together watching TV, Ivy looked over into their kitchen and saw an older woman wearing a black dress covered in black lace looking back at her. Ivy's husband Jeff noticed that his wife's attention was diverted from the TV, looked in the direction she was looking, and also saw the ghost of the woman standing in their kitchen.

Fully aware that his wife had seen ghosts in and around their home and fully aware of the train crash, he turned to Ivy and asked, "Do you know her?" Ivy answered, "No, but as long as she is in the kitchen she can do the dishes." Their son has seen the ghost of a little boy named Michael who likes to play with toys. On occasion Jeff has heard crying coming from their eldest boy's room when he was away with his grandmother. Jeff was a bit confused, and it was not until a few nights later, when he sneezed, that he heard a little child-like voice reply, "Bless you." Jeff has also seen a blond-haired boy in the kitchen as he was making dessert for their children. The boy slowly disappeared into thin air. Neighbors have reported that their battery operated toys, which have been turned off, will turn on and start moving and reacting as if someone is playing with them.

OLD TUCSON STUDIOS

As a child, my family would often vacation in Arizona, and when we were there, the one place I always wanted to visit was Old Tucson Studios. I enjoyed the reenactments, cowboys, and Hollywood magic nestled in the quiet Tucson Mountains. As a child it was one of my favorite places.

Columbia Pictures built the original studio in 1938, for their film *Arizona*; they needed to replicate 1860s Tucson for the movie. A few of the structures from the film are still standing in this world-famous studio. The studio went untouched for

a number of years until the mid-1940s, when old western films became extremely popular. During this time many films were made at the studio, including *The Bells of St. Mary's*, *The Last Round-Up*, *Winchester '73*, *The Last Outpost*, *Gunfight at the O.K. Corral*, *The Lone Ranger and the Lost City of Gold*, *Cimarron*, and *Rio Bravo*.

In 1959, it was purchased by Robert Shelton, who wanted to build an Old West style amusement park. He spent half a million dollars fixing the buildings and building areas for tourists to enjoy. During its heyday it received more than 500,000 visitors per year, and was the second most popular tourist destination in Arizona, second only to the Grand Canyon.

The morning of April 25, 1995, my mother woke me up very early and told me to come to her room to see the news. I saw Old Tucson Studios engulfed in flames. A fire had broken out in the studios, destroying most of the original buildings. There were not enough fire hydrants for the first firefighters on the scene to tackle the blaze.

With the help of Davis-Monthan Air Force Base and the Arizona Air National Guard it was under control in a number of hours, yet most of the studio was destroyed.

View of the church and train on the Old Tucson property.
Author Photo

It took twenty months for them to reconstruct the studios. During the reconstruction they widened the streets, and new sets were built instead of trying to recreate the sets destroyed in the blaze. The studios never fully recovered. They had to lessen their hours of operation and focus more on seasonal events, like their Halloween Nightfall event and their Wild Wild West Steampunk weekend.

After I moved to Bisbee and started my second business, Sweet Midnight, I was asked to vend and show off the Bisbee Mini Museum of the Bizarre during the Wild Wild West Steampunk Convention at Old Tucson Studios. I was so excited not only to be at the studios I loved as a child, but because I would be there at night, with very few other people around. After the guests have left and the sun starts to set the desert comes alive with strange sounds and eerie feelings. There is no doubt in my mind that Old Tucson Studios is haunted by spirits still lingering in the Tucson desert.

Some believe that there are several ghosts that haunt the old movie studio, though no one is certain why these spirits are there. There have been no recorded deaths at Old Tucson Studios, which causes us to believe that these spirits are either residual energy trapped in the historic locations, or they are spirits of people who were very fond of the old studios for one reason or another.

If you do an intense internet search, you can find articles from paranormal investigation groups that claim the old school house is said to be one of the most haunted buildings on the property. It is an old adobe building that is a replica of the first adobe schoolhouse built in Tucson in 1868. It is said to be haunted by a little girl who is the most talked about ghost at the studios.

When visitors walk into the schoolhouse, there is a feeling of being watched, and giggling of a child has also been heard. My friend, James Breen, claimed to see the head of the mannequin of a teacher move while he was in the schoolhouse after midnight during Wild Wild West Con. Though we asked employees about their ghostly experiences at the studios, not one mentioned the old schoolhouse.

There is a ghost that is said to haunt the Grand Palace Saloon, a restaurant and theatre, and one of the grandest buildings on the property. After you walk inside the Grand Palace Saloon you will get a feel of an Old West bar and theatre, with mounted taxidermy heads and grand velvet curtains. Guests have claimed to see a ghost child walking up the stairs to the second floor of the building.

Reported paranormal activity in the Grand Palace Saloon also includes a strange orange mist, as well as footsteps being heard when no one is in the building. Some claim to hear the footsteps on the empty stage, while others have heard them walk up and down the last row in the theatre. There is also a story of maintenance workers

View of the sun setting over the back of Old Tucson Studios in the Tucson Desert. *Author Photo*

Inside the haunted
Grand Palace Saloon
in Old Tucson Studios.
Author Photo

who were on a lift changing the light bulbs in the chandelier thirty-five feet in the air. They looked in the mirror behind the bar, only to see a ghost standing or floating right between them.

Rosa's Café is attached to the saloon and ghosts have been reported there, as well. Haunting activity includes the feeling of being watched and music turning on and off on the speakers in the café. Also attached to the Grand Palace Saloon is the ice cream parlor, where employees have seen a child dangling its legs over the freezer. Employees have described him as a playful spirit. They have also found a baby doll on the roof of the building, and no one knows where this doll came from or how it got there. Since all three of these places are one big building connected by corridors, the ghost of the little boy is most likely the one that haunts all three locations.

When we interviewed a few employees at the old studios, they told us stories of a little girl ghost named Josie who haunts the front cash office. Employees opening the office in the mornings will have to say, "Good morning" to Josie so she does not play with their cash box. If you do not say hello to her in the morning Josie will throw coins across the room. Josie can be heard laughing, and if you ask her to be quiet, she will immediately stop her giggle fit.

They also told us about a very mean, dark spirit that haunts the Bunker, also known as the Arizona Theatre. The Arizona Theatre is a strange structure that you enter through a dark tunnel that leads you down into what feels like an underground, cave-like room. The employees do not know what sort of entity is down there, but it is dark and malicious.

One of the employees and her husband were working on getting the studios ready for nightfall. Her husband asked her to help him in the Arizona Theatre and she refused, claiming that she did not like it down there and it creeped her out, and that she got an uneasy feeling when inside. Her husband finally convinced her to help him, and as she went down the eerie hallway into the center of the theatre she immediately had to leave the building, claiming that her chest was on fire.

After she was safely out of the structure, she looked at her neck, only to discover three long scratches going from the side of her neck down to her chest area. This is not the first report of women getting attacked there. Years prior a female security guard claimed she was pushed against the wall. She quit her job soon after the occurrence.

The ghost appears to hang out by the stage and sound booth. Reports of footsteps, heavy breathing, water running, objects moving, and a voice warning women to "get out" have also been heard. Females unaware of the paranormal activity have walked out of the theatre with bruises that they claim they did not have prior to walking into the building. The horses that live on site have been known to get spooked when walking around the building.

The old museum is said to have a ghost that lingers there. Years ago they used to show old John Wayne movies on loop on a TV set. One night, an employee went to turn off the TV and it turned right back on. He then unplugged the TV and it immediately came right back on.

Old Tucson Studios at night, when no one else is around, can be quite eerie. *Author Photo*

There is also believed to be the spirit of Jackson walking the grounds. Jackson used to be a custodian at Old Tucson Studios. He wore a cowboy hat and had long, beautiful blond hair. Jackson was a gentle soul who was very sad and depressed, and ended up committing suicide. Employees will catch glimpses of him by Chinese Alley. They will spot him going around the corner wearing his vest and hat, with his blond hair flowing behind him.

There is also believed to be a shadow man that has been seen walking the streets of Old Tucson after hours. Security guards have claimed to hear his footsteps, as well as the sound of spurs as he walks the abandoned streets.

The real question is why are these ghosts at the old studio? It is a question we might never know the answer to.

SKIN-WALKERS OF COPPER CREEK

Deep in the Galiuro Mountains, north and to the east of Tucson, is Copper Creek, an old abandoned copper mining town. All that remains are ruins of a few buildings. One of those buildings is the Sibley Mansion. Roy and Belle Sibley built the Sibley Mansion in 1908.

Roy managed his brother's mining interests. His wife was the first postwoman at the local post office, the remains of which can still be seen. Their mansion was 3,000 square feet and had two stone towers. After the mines were abandoned so was the mansion. Most of the structure was demolished and carted back to the town of Mammoth and sold as building supplies, yet the stones that were most likely too heavy to move are still there. The ghost of the building remains, but perhaps it is not the only ghost in Copper Creek. What my friends Wade and Michelle witnessed would most likely be classified as a shapeshifter.

On October 9, 2015, Wade and his wife Michelle decided to go camping along Copper Creek near Sibley Mansion. Locals in Mammoth refer to it as simply "the castle." Their adventure started out just like all of their camping adventures: they loaded up the UTVs and packed heavily for their camping pleasure.

They staged their UTVs near the Tucson Wash around noon and headed out on the twenty-five-mile drive to their camping location. Most people would ask why they did not stage closer and their answer was simple: they love the beautiful drive over the mountains and through the desert. They would always see something different every time they went through Copper Creek.

Once they passed through Mammoth and headed over the mountains on Copper Creek Road, their excitement levels were through the roof. They used all of their senses to soak in the beauty of southern Arizona. They crossed Copper Creek and headed down the right side of it; as they passed two water holding stations the atmosphere seemed to change, as if a dark cloud was following them. They simply chalked it up to just a weird feeling and pressed on.

They then took a very narrow trail alongside a deep ravine that led them to one of the old abandoned mines. Intrigued, they decided to stop and check out the area near the mine. They began to hear rocks fall in the distance; not very big rocks, but big enough for them to take notice and want to investigate. As they walked up the trail past the mine, Wade saw a shadow dart to the right around the corner of the trail, around the rocky ledge, and then out of view, so he decided to run after the shadow in an attempt to catch up to what he had just seen.

After running for about fifty yards he looked up, and saw what he believed to be a person dressed in all black about 300 yards in front of him. He described what he saw as "soul shaking terror." Wade's logical mind was telling him he was seeing things until his wife caught up to him and asked him what they were looking at and why was the person dressed in black. They stood there for about a minute staring at each other. The dark figure stared at them, just as they were staring at it. Wade adjusted his eyes, tilted his head, squatted, and stood back up, and the shadow figure never moved. As soon as Wade took a step forward the shadow figure seemed to squat down and began to multiply.

Both Wade and Michelle witnessed the figure form into two shadows which then started to crawl away from them and up the trail. They calmly turned around and walked back to their UTVs, almost in shock from their encounter. They decided that they would continue on to their campsite and still make the best out of their extremely peculiar experience.

Their adrenaline was pumping and their senses were on high alert, and both were scared beyond belief, but they rode their UTVs up the same trail where they had seen the shadow figure(s). When they got to the part of the trail where the shadow was standing, they could feel the dread overtake them. Wade described it as "being outside on a sunny day surrounded by happiness and then walking into a dark house filled with crying souls."

They approached the top of the ridge and decided to stop again and soak in the view, still on high alert and not saying much to each other. They both heard someone say, "Hey." They turned and looked at each other, and asked one another if they had said anything. At that same moment, before either one could answer the other, they heard a faint whispering. It sounded like there was a conversation taking place, but as intently as they were listening, all they could make out was gibberish. Then they started to hear the sound of falling rocks again. Michelle and Wade nervously laughed about this experience and pressed on to the Sibley Mansion.

As they headed down the ridge toward Copper Creek, they could see the Sibley Mansion poking up from the trees. They still felt the dark cloud following them, but not as close as it was forty-five minutes earlier, when the shadow figure showed its presence. They came to a partially opened black gate with a lock on it, but it was not locked to anything and it was not posted that they were not allowed in, so they pressed on.

They made their way down alongside the castle. As they scoped out an area for their camp, they noticed that the closer they got to the creek the more they felt out of place, as if they were in a different world. The trees and grass were lush from the monsoon season, which had just ended. They saw where others had made camp and thought it logical to set up in the same place. After their camp was set up they felt a little more relaxed about what they had experienced.

Wade and Michelle started to express their feelings about what they had just witnessed. They both admitted to each other that they were creeped out and felt the dread as they passed the location where they saw the shadow. As they were talking the sun dipped down past the mountains and it became eerily quiet and dark. They could feel the darkness surround them as night broke over the castle. They started a fire, hoping to lighten up the situation and warm their thoughts. At first it worked, until Michelle decided to take a picture of the fire in which a fiery, skeletal face appeared.

Immediately afterward they began to hear the same whispered conversations they had heard just a few hours prior. They felt as if something was in the dark, watching them, waiting for them. With unspoken words Michelle and Wade decided to pack up and leave. In their haste to get out of camp they forgot their tent, along with some cooking utensils. They carefully drove up the ridge line to the black gate, which was now closed and locked. They questioned how a gate that just a few hours prior had been open was now closed with chain and lock. Luckily they had four-wheel-drive on both of the UTVs and they went around the gate. They drove back down the trails alongside Copper Creek feeling as if they were being chased by the darkness the whole time.

Wade started to feel better the closer they got to Mammoth. Once they got to the Tucson Wash, Wade claimed that his soul felt as if they were out of the woods and home free, except they were not. They began to see lights approaching ahead along the hilltop just past where their truck was parked. They got to the truck and the lights were now at a standstill, as if they were waiting for them. They loaded up the truck and made their way toward the lights. They rounded the corner and the lights were no longer there. The only thing that was where the light had been was a cross marking the spot where someone had driven off the road.

Wade and Michelle state that night truly changed their lives and opened their minds to the endless possibilities of the different spirits that surround us. Wade said:

> BE IT A SPIRIT GUIDE LEADING YOU IN THE RIGHT DIRECTION OR A DEVIOUS SPIRIT LEADING YOU DOWN A PATH OF DESPAIR, ALL YOU HAVE TO DO IS LISTEN WITH YOUR MIND AND SEE WITH YOUR SOUL. IT IS UP TO YOU TO DECIDE WHICH PATH YOU WANT TO TAKE. AND FROM WHAT WE SAW AND HEARD THAT NIGHT, WE CHOSE TO GO HOME, AND WE STILL DO NOT MISS THE TENT OR COOKING ITEMS THAT WERE LEFT BEHIND.

MINIATURE GHOST

My favorite haunting in Tucson is also the tiniest haunting that I have ever come across. The ghost resides in the hidden gem that is the Mini Time Machine, Museum of Miniatures.

This museum is filled with artisan made miniature houses, gypsy wagons, and shadow boxes and is sure to delight your inner child.

There is one house in particular that is showcased as soon as you walk into the museum's History Gallery. The house looks like a three-story colonial home painted white with brown window shutters and brown trim—very typical of a home you would find on the east coast. The miniature house has a beautiful, rounded porch, and is even landscaped with a vegetable garden, flowers, trees, and bushes. The landscaping alone took artist Era Pearce three years to complete. There are rabbits and little foxes, as well as a family of pigs playing in the mud.

This extraordinary miniature house was built by artist John Bellemy in the 1800s, and was a replica of his home in Massachusetts. The miniature was originally built as a gift for his daughter. It ended up in the hands of collectors, who added electricity to the home. There are replica electric Tiffany desk lamps in the house that would not have been accurate to the time period, but we can overlook this inaccuracy due to the splendor and craftsmanship that went into the entire piece. The owner of the museum, Pat Arnell, restored the house after she took ownership of it.

The most fascinating part of this miniature is that it is haunted. A miniature house having a miniature ghost seems insane, though if you ask the staff who work there or the docents who volunteer their time, they will tell you that objects in the house will move. There are stories that prior to the house relocating to the museum it was in Pat Arnell's home. She would notice chairs in the miniature office would be moved from where she left them, as well as a toast rack moving from the stove to beneath the table on the floor. There is even a sign on the wall adjacent to the miniature house describing the miniature poltergeist.

So if you are in Tucson, we highly recommend visiting the Mini Time Machine Museum of Miniatures to try to get a glimpse at what could be the tiniest ghost in existence.

CHAPTER 9
ARIZONA CITY

Arizona City sits halfway between Tucson and Phoenix off the I-10 freeway. Developers decided to start building in this location due to its proximity to the Sawtooth Mountains and the abundance of deep, pure water found there. It soon turned into a typical suburban neighborhood with stucco houses that each resembled one another and a golf course that brought in snow birds and locals alike.

ARIZONA CITY UFO ABDUCTION

In 1981, my friend Barry was living with his parents in a brand-new housing development in Arizona City. There were homes on his block still being built, so the already built homes had empty lots between and behind them. It was in one of these empty lots that Barry and his friend Tom, who lived across town and would come over to Barry's house to hang out, found a bush that had space underneath it to use as the perfect fort.

They used chicken wire and boards they found to enclose their fort, and it was there that they spent a lot of their free time. They would ride their BMX bikes through the vacant lots to their fort and spend their days and sometimes nights there. Their fort was only about 200 yards away from Barry's parents' house, but to them it felt like miles.

One night during the summer of 1981, Tom and Barry decided to go to their fort around eight o'clock in the evening, as Barry remembers it being very dark out. They rode their BMX bikes into the desert to their fort, and not long afterward saw what appeared to be a group of bright white lights one hundred feet directly above them. The lights started to get closer and closer until they were forty feet above them and then twenty feet above them.

The lights made a strange pattern on the bottom of what appeared to be a hovering craft. The boys heard no sound and only felt air swooshing past them, yet could not hear it. The last thing Barry recalled was jumping into a thorny bush clinging to his BMX bike for dear life, and with good reason, as he was about to have a close encounter of the third kind.

Barry was transported into the UFO for an unknown amount of time. He remembers very little of the experience, but did take home a souvenir. It is not uncommon for UFO abductees to be left with a scar known as a post alien abduction body mark. Barry was left with two scars: one on the back of his neck and one on the base of his spine. The body marks look like little white dots aligned in a row.

Strangely, Barry remembers very little of the night, including what the inside of the craft looked like, seeing the UFO leave, talking to Tom about their experience, or going home. It was as if it never happened, though this is not uncommon in abduction cases, as the human brain tends to forget traumatic experiences. Most who have a close encounter of the third kind experience time loss and loss of memory of the experience. They are left with a foggy recollection of what occurred if at all, and it is not until later that they start to piece the experience together, sometimes through hypnotherapy.

As for Barry, he completely forgot about the experience until he was a teenager and one of his friends asked him if he had ever seen a UFO. Upon hearing the question the memories of his fort and jumping into the thorny bush started to flood back into his consciousness.

As years passed Tom and Barry went their separate ways, losing contact with one another; to this day they have not had contact. Barry did remain in contact with the girl who lived across the street, Nikki. Nikki and Barry worked at the Arizona City Country Club together. When Barry asked her if she remembered seeing any UFOs in or around Arizona City, she claimed that the country club members would regularly talk about the UFOs they had spotted. She acted as if it was a typical conversation that occurred at the country club, and even though Barry also worked there, he had no recollection of hearing any stories of UFOs between the members. He believes that his subconscious chose not to remember them. To this day Barry states he is not afraid of UFOs or aliens, but fears what others will think of him after hearing his story, so we changed his name to keep his identity secret.

HIGH MOUNTAINS

HIGH MOUNTAINS BIGFOOT

In 2008, our friends Jessy and Doyle were camping and elk hunting in the High Mountains. Jessy had arrived at the campground to get everything set up prior to Doyle's arrival. Jessy set up the entire campground, and the night before Doyle was to arrive was asleep in his tent. He was awoken by noises outside, and his tent then suddenly began to move; it appeared a creature was tangled in the tent line.

As the creature was getting more agitated by being caught up in the tent, it started twisting and turning, twisting up the tent with Jessy inside it. Jessy got a quick glimpse of a creature standing upright on two feet. After the creature freed itself from the tent and tent lines, Jessy, too afraid to get out of the tangled tent, braved the night inside the mess.

When morning arrived, he felt his courage return enough to exit the tent. In doing so, he noticed that the creature had moved the tent, with him inside, ten feet from where it was originally pitched. Jessy took the tent, untangled it, repitched it, made himself coffee, and was smoking a cigarette when Doyle drove in to the campground. Doyle got out of his truck, and Jessy looked up from his coffee and said, "God Damn Yeti," and recounted the story of the previous night. After Doyle, shocked from the story his friend had just told him, took his bow and arrows out of his truck and was starting to settle into camp, two Native American police officers stopped by to see how their guests were doing.

They asked if anything strange had happened in recent days. Doyle gave Jessy a look that without saying any words Jessy understood, but he refused to tell the Native Americans what had happened to him the night prior. The Native Americans started telling the men that within the last few months many Elk trophy hunters were getting scared and leaving the area. These trophy hunters pay the reservation anywhere from $18,000–$25,000 dollars for the opportunity to hunt elk in that area, and they were getting so scared they were leaving empty-handed. They then explained that the Yeti was scaring men off.

They asked Jessy and Doyle again if they had seen anything. It was at this point that Jessy realized that they would not think he was as crazy as he initially thought and told them in detail what happened to him the night before. The Native American police officers explained that the Yeti had been in the area for as long as their tribe and that they had never hurt anyone, yet are extremely curious creatures, and especially like tents.

Jessy and Doyle would not let a bunch of hairy, smelly, curious yetis stop them from their good time. They braved the potential of getting their camp destroyed by the unseen beasts, and it was not until the end of their trip that they once again encountered the Yeti.

Doyle had gone out with his bow and arrow and had shot an elk that was atop a steep hill on the second to last day of their excursion. He decided to let it bleed out and would return early the next morning to claim his kill. The next morning the elk was gone. There was blood where the animal had bled out, but no blood trail. It was clear that the animal had died due to the major blood loss, yet it had been taken from where Doyle had shot it with his arrow. The elk was estimated to be around 600 pounds and would have to have been physically lifted, since it was on a hill and there was no way a truck could have driven up a slope that steep. There were no animal tracks, no entrails, and except for the blood pool, no evidence the elk was ever there.

Doyle decided to head seven miles to the Artesian Wells, where the elk would go to drink, in an attempt to acquire one more prize before they packed up camp and started to head back home. As he was in the brush waiting for the most opportune moment to shoot an elk, he heard a loud, high-pitched scream. He heard what sounded like a two-legged creature running through the bushes, breaking twigs and branches in the process. At that exact moment Jessy came driving up in his truck, and Doyle believes that the vehicle scared the creature, because he then heard the loud, fast steps that were running through the bushes get farther and farther away from him.

A few years later Doyle was on his computer as his kids were in the other room watching television. He was not paying much attention to the show his kids were watching, until he heard a loud, high-pitched scream come from the TV set. The scream was identical to the one he heard while at the Artesian Wells. He got up from the computer desk and walked into the room to see what the kids were watching, only to discover they were watching a show on Bigfoot.

YUMA

Yuma, Arizona, sits in the corner of the state, with California to the west and Mexico to the south. It was an excellent site for a city due to the Colorado River, which runs right alongside the town. At one point the Colorado River becomes very narrow and made an ideal crossing point for people who were dreaming of riches during the California Gold Rush.

After merchants eventually saw the potential in this area the city began to grow. It changed names a few times, and over the years saw many businesses come and go, from steamboats that would bring supplies to the prison that would house inmates. Though Yuma is most famous for its climate—being the sunniest spot in the entire world—the hottest temperature it has ever reached was 124 degrees in 1995. We recommend visiting between November and April, when the temperatures do not get higher than ninety degrees. Today Yuma has a Marine base, a border patrol station, a beautiful historic shopping district, and a plethora of ghosts.

YUMA COUNTY COURTHOUSE

The first Yuma County Courthouse was originally built in 1900. After a fire devastated much of the building it had to be rebuilt in 1928. The building had an addition built next to it, since the original building was too small to meet the high demands of the court system in Yuma as the city began to grow. The original courthouse still houses offices, a law library, and courtrooms. When I went to visit the courthouse after hearing rumors of it being haunted, it took talking to a lot of court employees before we were escorted to the office of Ceasar Fazz, a collections supervisor and paranormal aficionado.

Mr. Fazz is no stranger to ghosts. When he was a detective in Yuma in the early '90s he lived at 221 W. 21st Street as a single bachelor. After a long day of work he would sit and watch TV and out of the corner of his eye would see a shadow of a small child peering from around the corner. After he met his wife and she moved into the house with him, she claimed to also have seen this shadow creature. A few years later they started a family and eventually moved out of the house. One of their children claims that as a child they saw the shadow ghost as well. After they moved out of that house they never saw the ghost again, and felt sad to have left it behind.

We sat down in Mr. Fazz's office as he took photos off his wall and pulled articles out of his desk drawer about Adolph Teichman. Teichman was a gentleman who lived in the building as a night watchman and bailiff. Teichman was believed to have died on Christmas morning in 1949, inside his loft above the top floor of the building where he lived. The judge at the time was coming to the courthouse to pick Teichman up to take him back to his house for Christmas dinner when his lifeless body was found. Teichman was buried in Yuma Cemetery in an unmarked grave.

Though Teichman died and his body was buried, most employees believe that his spirit remains in the building he lived in and watched over. Many do not enjoy

working at night for fear that they might encounter his ghost walking up and down the halls, checking on locked doors, and opening them as well. Employees have heard footsteps and keys rattling, and when they go into the hallway to see who it is of course no one is there.

Mr. Fazz told us that in the break room next to his office Teichman likes to play jokes on the ladies as they are taking their lunch break. The break room has a closet directly to the left when you walk in, with a motion sensor light that you need to physically wave your hand in front of to get the light in the closet to go on. When the female employees go into the break room for lunch they will usually turn off the lights in the room, sit down at one of the round tables, turn on the TV, enjoy their meal, and relax until their hour break is up. However, sometimes it is hard to relax with a ghost in the room with you.

Teichman's spirit will turn the closet light on when only females are in the room taking their lunch break. Since the sensor to the closet light is inside the closet, and you have to physically put your hand in the closet and wave it around to trigger the sensor, it is always blamed on the ghost.

When we were researching the ghost stories, Mr. Fazz was nice enough to take us up to the storage area they refer to as the "Crow's Nest," where Adolph Teichman lived and died. At the time I was not allowed to walk on my left foot and was on a knee cart. Mr. Fazz unlocked the door leading up to the old loft. I got off my knee cart and we left it by the locked door. My husband and Mr. Fazz walked up the stairs ahead of me while I slowly limped my way up, being careful not to put weight on my left foot. During the climb an eerie feeling came over me, as if something did not want us to be there.

We made our way to the loft space and Mr. Fazz pointed out the trigger object he put for Teichman's ghost to play with. It was a small bottle of correction fluid marked so that Mr. Fazz would know if it had been moved. We discussed the building, the city of Yuma, and the Old Bisbee Ghost Tours, hoping that the ghost would join in the conversation. Mr. Fazz was explaining to us that he has never seen anything and wanted to experience some paranormal activity firsthand. I explained that when he least expected it, it would happen. After taking a few photos we decided it was time to descend the staircase.

This time I led the way and the men followed me. When we got to the door, Mr. Fazz took my cart up a couple of the stairs to allow us to get the door open. My husband pulled on the door but it was locked. There is a sensor on the door that you trigger when you are standing in front of it, much like the sensor in the break room. When it is triggered from the inside, it is supposed to automatically unlock so no one gets locked in. The sensor was on and the light on it was green, indicating that it sensed us and was unlocked, yet the door would not open.

My husband and Mr. Fazz switched places. My husband held my scooter on the stairs and Mr. Fazz tried to open the doors, but to no avail. My husband handed his phone to Mr. Fazz so he could call someone in the building to try to save us when I said out loud, "Mr. Teichman, could you please open the door for us." Still the door would not open. As Mr. Fazz was starting to dial a number I asked out loud one more time, "Mr. Teichman, can you please unlock the door for us," and before Mr. Fazz had time to finish dialing the number he tried the door one more time and it opened. I turned to Mr. Fazz and said, "See! Happens when you least expect it."

Mr. Fazz and I became Facebook friends, and he informed us that a judge had granted us permission to do a paranormal investigation of the courthouse. November 9, 2016, was the night we were allowed to do the investigation. I decided this was also the perfect time to interview other employees of the courthouse to see what, if any, paranormal activity they had experienced while working there.

Mr. Fazz arranged for one of the prosecutors and his receptionist who worked on the first floor to allow me to interview them. The receptionists told me that when they are alone in the office they would hear shuffling papers and the squeaking of a chair, as if someone was sitting in one of the chairs in the office. They said the TV in the office would go on and change the channel to a station with static and white noise.

Distant muffled voices can be heard when they are alone, as well as strange knocks on the wall. When one of the employees was working alone on the weekend she heard the door to the women's bathroom opening and then slamming closed. She went to ask them to keep it down and discovered that no one was there. The lights in the women's room would turn off by themselves as well. There is also a story of a woman who was in the ladies' room when she had her backside pinched by the ghost. The prosecutor had a heart-to-heart with the ghost and told it that it was allowed to stay as long as it did not scare or hurt the staff. They said that they were the boss, not the ghost. They also stated that most of the noises and knocks they hear come from the prosecutor's office, which used to be a clerk's office. When it was a clerk's office the computers would turn on and off by themselves.

One day the girls were working in their office when they decided to play with the Snapchat app on their phone. One girl was snapchatting and using the photo filter with a flower halo. She then noticed that the app recognized another face floating above hers and added the flower halo to that one. The video was saved to her backup device, and when she paused the video to take a closer look there appeared to be a translucent face floating above hers.

Recently children's voices, giggling, and sounds of playing have been heard on the first floor by the custodians.

Cecil was a retired custodian who used to work at the Yuma Courthouse for twelve years. He was the man who actually took apart Adolph Teichman's residence in the "Crows Nest" in 1990. Prior to that, the only thing that was removed from Teichman's room was the cot. During the time when Cecil was taking apart the shower, he felt as if he was not alone and was constantly being watched. After that, and during the years that followed, a lot of paranormal activity occurred in the building. He said that sounds of children running up and down the halls were what scared him the most.

He told us that one evening, around midnight, he had walked in the front door on the first floor at the bottom of the stairs and saw two black orbs float from the second floor down to the first floor and then disappear into a wall. He said the first black orb was bigger than the one behind it. He said that the ghosts would also call out his name. He went to find out who was calling his name and when no one was there he quickly left and found safety in his truck.

In the break room where the lights turn off Cecil claimed to hear knocking on the windows, as well as witnessing the door to the break room open all the way by itself. He asked a fellow employee who was also working that night to check the room to make sure no one was in there, and sure enough, the room was completely empty. He stated that the ghosts would also unplug his radio that he used to drown out the noises the ghosts would make. Once he heard his music stop and he went downstairs to figure out why. The plug had been taken out of the wall and the electrical cord was wrapped around the radio.

Cecil also told us stories of what is now referred to as the "dungeon," which is an area of the courthouse that is used for storage. There is what appears to be an old jail door that is locked, and beyond that is the foundation of the building. Cecil told us that this area used to be where his tools were kept, and claimed that one of his coworkers witnessed boxes being moved in the "dungeon" by unseen hands.

Another employee was in there laying tile when they were remodeling, when all of a sudden the lights turned off. Thinking one of his coworkers was playing a joke on him, he started to yell for someone to turn the lights back on because he was still working. There was no response. He got up and found that the light he was using to illuminate the area where he was working had been unplugged. He plugged it back in and went back to work. The lights abruptly went off again. Again thinking someone was playing a joke on him, he went back out to find that the light had been unplugged again. He plugged it back in again and continued laying down tile. Suddenly the tiles he was laying down started to be thrown and were crashing all around him. At that point he got up and left the area.

Cecil was working one evening, picking up trash with one of the county prisoners who help provide inexpensive labor to the courthouse. They were headed up to the crows nest where Adolph Teichman used to live when the prisoner stopped. Cecil urged him to hurry up because they had a lot of work to do. The prisoner still refused. When Cecil asked him why he would not go up the stairs, the prisoner responded in a deep southern accent, "There is somebody walking up them steps, and there ain't no one there."

An inmate once helping Cecil claimed that someone grabbed him and pulled him from behind. He jumped back, ready to punch whomever it was that did it, and when he turned around no one was there. One of the current security guards had a similar story, stating that in the middle of the day, when it was still light out, he felt as if someone grabbed his gun. His partner was standing feet behind him. He asked his partner why he grabbed his gun and his partner responded that he had not.

As we toured the building with Cecil, we discovered that there had been a lot of renovations done to the building. Most of the stairs and offices that used to be there had since been changed or taken out. The entire layout of the building is different than the way it used to be. As we made our way around the building we ended up in the dungeon. We entered through the old jail door. The room we entered had a few of the old light fixtures in it. There was layered sandstone and what appeared to be old rebar sticking out of the ground. It seemed older than that which would have been used to construct the building. There were a couple concrete steps

The staircase where Cecil saw two black
orbs floating. *Author Photo*

that led to a very small hallway that we needed to crouch down in to get through. That hallway opened up into another, bigger room, where there were pipes that we assumed led to the building and a dirt floor that had been dug out to about eight feet deep.

Across from the entrance to this room there was a brick wall with a closed-off double door. Where this door leads is unknown, and did not appear to be part of the original building. The red brick wall appeared to be out of place and did not match any of the bricks we could find on the current building, nor any of the bricks from old photos of the original structure. There was another room in the back of that one and my husband ventured into it. The only thing he saw in the second room was what we believe to be the molds used to make the ceilings in the staircases.

We started our investigation on the first floor in the main hallway, right below the staircase where Cecil saw two black orbs floating down the stairs, hoping to catch evidence of the children running up and down the halls. Though we did not get any hits on our KII meters or EMF detectors, it appears we got the sound of what seems to be a ball being bounced for a couple seconds. We could also hear what seemed to be footsteps, but for only a moment or two. I also swore that I heard giggling, except no one else in the area confirmed that they also heard it.

Then we went up to the crows nest to continue the investigation. As we walked up the stairs our KII meters went off, a strong indication that there was a presence in there with us. At one point we saw the door to what used to be Adolph Teichman's living quarters close by itself.

Not long after the door closed Mr. Fazz, who was standing on the staircase, started to hear knocking. He could not tell where it was coming from or who was making it. He ran into the storage room to get my attention and I ran by the stairs in time to hear one loud knock. I thought it was the door sensor going off, but Mr. Fazz told me it was a completely different noise, which we later discovered to be true. At the same time our KII meters started going off on the staircase.

Even though we did a paranormal investigation in the building and caught what we hope is real paranormal activity, the mystery of the ghosts that haunt the Yuma County Courthouse has not yet been solved. We really want to discover who the children are that are said to haunt the first floor and why they are there. We are also curious why there is the strange wall and door in the dungeon.

Yuma County Territorial Prison

The Yuma Territorial Prison was built on a hill overlooking the Colorado River in 1875, and had a budget of $25,000. In 1876, construction began, and prisoners were used to help construct the building they would soon occupy. The prisoners carried the rock from the hills and constructed the adobe walls. There was a solitary hole that was constructed out of these rocks. The only light that came in was from the iron door when it was opened and a small ventilation hole in the ceiling. There was an iron ring on the floor for inmates to be chained to, ensuring that they were unable to escape. This was a place where prisoners who broke the rules were taken after they were stripped down to nothing more than their underwear.

This dark, dingy cell was referred to as the "Dark Cell." Construction on the prison took about five years and soon after, the prisoners were escorted into their new home. It was in service for only thirty-three years, but during that time 3,069 prisoners were incarcerated. Out of those 3,069 prisoners there were twenty women, some of whom were imprisoned for polygamy.

Yuma Territorial Prison was referred to as the "Country Club" because there was a library, hospital, air conditioning, electricity, and a craft market where prisoners made and sold their handmade picture frames, jewelry, boxes, and canes.

According to the website, 112 prisoners died while at Yuma Territorial Prison. Eight were shot while trying to escape, six committed suicide, five died in work accidents, two died at the hands of another prisoner, and only one was executed by Yuma County.

After the prison closed in 1909 due to overcrowding, the vacant buildings were used to house Yuma Union High School. Their football team is appropriately called the "Criminals" and their merchandise can be purchased from the store called the "Cell Block."

After the high school was relocated, the prison's superintendent's house was used as the county hospital. In 1916, there was a flood that wiped out most of Yuma. Residents looked to the old prison for building supplies. They took the buildings apart to reuse materials to rebuild their homes and businesses.

During the Depression people down on their luck used the jail cells as makeshift homes. Families would pile into a cell to protect themselves from the elements until happier times were among them again. They had shelter and water, which was what they needed to get by and survive day-to-day. In 1939, the squatters were evicted, and a year later the museum that welcomes visitors to this day was built on the site of the old prison mess hall.

Today visitors can tour Yuma Territorial Prison to learn about its historic past, and if you do, you might run into the spirits of prisoners who never left.

There are said to be three haunted locations in the prison: Cell 14, the dark cell, and the gift shop. When my husband and I planned one of our yearly trips to Los Angeles, I requested we take Interstate 8 so we could stop by Yuma Territorial Prison and see if we could encounter any of the ghosts. I had read that one of the ghosts will pinch guests wearing the color red, so my husband wore a red t-shirt and I wore a red dress. It was an extremely hot day at the end of July when we went. Very few people were visiting due to the excessive heat.

We paid for our tickets in the gift shop and made our way to the museum, which used to be the old mess hall. Luckily the museum was air-conditioned. It was full of exhibits detailing the daily lives of prisoners. One of the prison's volunteer tour guides spotted us and asked us if we would like a private tour of the grounds. Of course we said yes, and he took us outside to what used to be a cell block of the prison. It was a hallway with cells on either side. The doorways to the cells were arched, and there were heavy metal doors with a special hinge with a rod on them.

The hinges and pole were used so that one guard could resist the strength of multiple prisoners had there been an attempted break-out. As we walked down the corridor and heard the tales of daily life at the prison, we soon arrived at the last cell in the row, cell number 14. As we approached the cell our guide put his hands together and said a little prayer to himself. We asked him why he did that and he stated it was "to protect us from the spirit which lingers in cell 14."

The cell seemed darker than the other cells we passed, and we felt extremely cold air making its way from inside the cell to where we were standing just next to the cell door. The spirit that is believed to haunt this cell is that of John Ryan. Ryan was convicted of "an act against nature," which in the early 1900s was how they referred to rape. Ryan was disliked not only by the guards, but also by the other prisoners. He felt that his only way out of prison was death. He committed suicide by hanging himself in his cell. He used the blankets in his cell to carry out his deed.

My paranormal advisor, Christy, had a chilling experience outside cell 14. She wrote down her experience for me:

ABOUT FOUR YEARS AGO I WAS AT YUMA TERRITORIAL PRISON, BEING LED AROUND IN A TOUR GROUP. IT WAS AN EXTREMELY HOT DAY, AND ALL I WAS WORRIED ABOUT WAS FINDING SOME SHADE OR GOING BACK INTO THE AIR-CONDITIONED MUSEUM. AS WE WALKED BY CELL 14, A MAN'S ARMS FLEW OUT OF THE CELL BARS AND I JUMPED OUT OF THE WAY SO HE COULD NOT GRAB ME. MY FRIEND WAS AS SHOCKED AS I WAS, AS I EVEN LET OUT A LITTLE YELP AS I JUMPED OUT OF THE WAY. WHEN I LOOKED BACK AT THE CELL I SAW A MAN HANGING. I AM PSYCHIC, AND SPIRITS LIKE TO SHOW ME HOW THEY DIED. I WAS VERY TAKEN ABACK AND SHOCKED. I HAD NO IDEA ANYTHING LIKE THAT WOULD HAPPEN, AS I DID NOT RESEARCH ANY OF THE PRISON'S HISTORY PRIOR TO GOING ON THE TOUR.

WHEN I HAD TIME TO DO RESEARCH, I FOUND OUT THAT CELL 14 IS STILL RUMORED TO BE HAUNTED BY JOHN RYAN. HE DIED ON MAY 6, 1903, AFTER COMMITTING SUICIDE BY HANGING HIMSELF IN HIS CELL. HE WAS NOT WELL LIKED BECAUSE HE WAS CONVICTED FOR ACTS AGAINST NATURE, WHICH IS NOW CLASSIFIED AS RAPE.

The dark cell is also believed to be haunted. Guests visiting the dark cell while wearing the color red are believed to aggravate the ghosts and entice them to interact. Dressed in our red clothes, my husband and I waited for all the guests to leave the dark cell, after which we were the only ones there.

The eeriness that overcomes your entire body is hard to describe. The feeling of being watched is undeniable; perhaps it could have been from the numerous bats

A row of cells that still remain
at the old Yuma Territorial
Prison. *Author Photo*

that roost in the dark cell, or perhaps it was the souls of prisoners long gone that were watching our every move. The dark cell's air is cold and stale, and the only light is from a portal in the ceiling and from the hall leading from the entrance. There is no doubt that even if it was not haunted, being inside the cell gives you an uneasy feeling.

Though we were hoping to get pinched, neither my husband nor I did. Our tour guide told us that photos of ghostly apparitions have been photographed near the cell. He also told us a story of a reporter who requested to spend the night in the cell. She asked to be chained up to experience what the prisoners experienced. After only a few hours she started to freak out and requested to be unchained and taken out.

The gift shop is also said to be haunted. Many employees believe it is haunted by a little girl. It is strange that a child would be there, since it was a prison. During the Depression the prison was used as a shelter for families and individuals that did not have a home. Is it possible that one of these families had a little girl? Is it also possible that she could have died while living at the prison? Though there is no historic evidence to prove this theory, many people believe the little girl ghost drowned in the nearby Colorado River. She is said to play with the change kept in the register in the gift shop, sometimes flinging the coins across the room with her unseen hands. Though mischievous, she rarely scares anyone, as it is obvious she just wants to have fun.

Some might be scared of the ghosts and others might venture to the old prison to experience them. Either way, it is a very interesting and historic place; we just recommend visiting during the cooler months.

THE YUMA PUMP HOUSE

This is no ordinary family home; it must be one of the most unique homes in Arizona. It was built in 1921, to provide water to the local farms throughout Yuma County by pumping water from the Colorado River, which runs alongside the building, through gigantic turbines. After more modern methods of transporting water were implemented the building sat vacant. The building might have been vacated by the living, but the dead never left.

In the 1970s, it was renovated and opened as a restaurant. It was during this time that people started to report paranormal activity. In the dining hall, when guests were eating, employees and customers alike would notice people sitting in the room who looked like transients. They would disappear as they were approached to be asked to leave. Many believe that these apparitions are the residual energy from men who helped build the pump house, as they were always dirty from working so hard and would usually be seen wearing overalls; if you did not know any better they could be confused with transients. Perhaps

Author Rene Harper venturing into the dark cell. *Photo by James Harper*

it was the hauntings that caused the restaurant to close a few years after it originally opened.

In 1984, Carol Engler-Foree bought the building and renovated it to meet current residential housing codes. She raised her family in the house, which she converted into a beautiful and extremely unique home. After twenty years Carol moved out and allowed the house to be used as a delinquent home for troubled boys. One boy set the house on fire. Most of the inside of the house was burned and had to be completely remodeled. Though no one was harmed in the fire, Carol spent years refurbishing the house and upon completion moved back in. Over the years Carol sold and rebought the pump house four times.

Though the residual energy of the men who built the original pump house may still be imprinted on the building, there is evidence of an intelligent haunting that still lingers there. Many believe it is that of a worker who was killed during the construction of the building. If you believe campfire stories that have been told from generation to generation, the legend says that a worker leaned the wrong way on a pipe that had a razor sharp edge. He slipped and got decapitated as his neck hit the pipe edge.

Those wishing to scare little kids elaborate on the story, stating that the head was washed away when the pump was turned on. Others claim that to cover up the evidence of his death they buried the body in the cement walls near the large cylinders that used to pump the water. The real story is most likely a little less dramatic. Though we found no historical data to back it up, many believe that a gentleman who was working on the pump house got injured and died on the property.

I found Carol on Facebook and told her I was writing this book. I asked if she could share some of her ghostly experiences that happened in the house with me. Her stories were fascinating and started thirty years ago with her general contractor, Norm. He was downstairs in the "tubes," sealing them off so that animals like snakes and rats and transients would not be able to climb through the tubes and into the home, when he heard the pull chain toilet flush.

Chain toilets are extremely loud when they flush and it startled Norm, because he knew he was the only one there at the time. He went tearing out of the tube like a bat out of hell to see if anyone else had entered the building. He ran into the toilet area and saw no one was there, except that the pull chain on the toilet was swinging all by itself.

When you walk into the pump house through its huge glass doors, there is a room directly to the right. When the building was a restaurant (around 1978), the office was in this room, which is where the master bedroom is now. The door to the then-office was locked, but the adding machine started running all by itself, as if an unseen employee was working on the numbers for the restaurant and helping the manager. The adding machine did not stop running until it ran out of paper.

A view of the pump house from
the driveway in Yuma, Arizona.
Author Photo

There are multiple stories from guests who did not know one another who used to frequent the restaurant. On different occasions they told Carol similar stories of apparitions being seen upstairs in the loft, which used to be a dining area. They told her that lights would turn on and off. Lit candles would float in a bouncing manner down the staircase, and luckily they did not set the building on fire. These encounters were told by different people who were at the restaurant at different times, yet all their stories were quite similar.

In the mid-1990s, in the master bedroom, they had a door that could only lock from the inside. One day, out of the clear blue, the door locked by itself from the inside when no one was there. Carol and her husband had to crawl in through a window from the balcony to get the door unlocked.

On another occasion, Carol's mother was babysitting her grandchildren in the early 1990s, and all of a sudden she heard banging, rattling of chains, and clanging. She told the ghost out loud, "Shut up, I'm trying to sleep." At that moment all the noises instantly stopped.

Carol's daughter's room was downstairs, in the part of the house that used to hold all the heavy equipment for the machines to pump water. The daughter said that one night all her stuffed animals started flying off the three shelves above her bed. She did not see or hear anyone, she only saw the stuffed animals start to fly from the shelves, which were seven feet high off the floor of her bedroom.

Julio, their remodeling contractor, told Carol the workers were afraid of working at the pump house because of it being haunted. She also claims to have had a picture of a devil that was drawn on one of the walls downstairs.

Carol had a baby shower at the house years ago and one of the guests, who had never been there before, asked her if the house had any ghosts. Carol responded, stating to her that it was such a curious question. The woman said she saw a little girl ghost downstairs. This woman was the second person who had not been at the building before but had told Carol they saw a ghost of a little girl.

Roni Miles is Carol's twin sister. Her son slept at the pump house when he was a small child, around four years old. He came up the stairs the next morning very sleepy and was whining that the ghost wanted to play and would not let him sleep during the night. To this day neither Carol's sister nor her son will sleep downstairs. When the sister comes to visit she sleeps in Carol's room and her husband sleeps downstairs. Her nephew will only stay in a hotel.

Carol explained that she has had a couple paranormal investigation groups try to find the ghosts in the pump house. One group of young investigators in their early twenties claimed the spirits that reside in the building told them, "The ghost said Norm and Ben did a great job on the house." Norm was the first contractor on the house and Ben was the second. Carol does not believe there was any way the investigators would have known who Norm and Ben were.

In November 2016, Carol and her husband invited my husband and I to the pump house to give us a tour. As you approach the house from the road, you notice right away that it is a unique home unlike any other. Entering through its huge glass and iron doors, you enter a huge, open floor plan with ceilings so high I had to question how they changed the light bulbs. There is a staircase with a loft and a huge kitchen.

The open floor plan includes a double fireplace and magnificent windows that allow the entire house to be lit by natural sunlight. Carol took me downstairs to the area where the extra bedrooms and her husband's "man cave" are. This was the area of the house that used to hold the equipment that ran the pumps. When the building was a restaurant the downstairs was used as a bar area.

The walls downstairs were made with twenty-six-inch-thick poured concrete and rebar. As we approached the room that used to be her daughter's bedroom at the end of a long hallway, Carol remarked, "That's interesting." As I looked in the room, it appeared that a sliding closet door that was on tracks had been removed from the tracks and had fallen over, knocking over a stained-glass lamp that was on a bedside table, though the lamp was not broken, which I thought was odd. It also appeared to have hit a framed picture on the wall that was set askew, yet the glass frame was not damaged at all. It was as if it was knocked over with such care as to not cause it to break. Without a second glance Carol returned the closet door to the original location from which it fell and put the lamp back in its place, as if this was something that was not out of the ordinary.

She continued to explain that this particular room was the one with the most paranormal activity and is the one where her daughter witnessed her stuffed animals being thrown off the shelf by unseen hands. She said that her daughter would not talk about the different occurrences that have happened in her childhood bedroom.

Carol stated that one time her son and his girlfriend were staying in the room, visiting for the weekend with their pet dog. Out of the blue the dog started growling at the door leading to the hallway. When they opened the door there was a definite cold spot. Others have claimed to have witnessed poltergeist activity in the room as well.

After we left the bedroom, we walked down the hallway to the opposite end of the house, where the tubes are still located. As you enter the man cave you can see a gigantic round hole in the wall, which is one of the tubes. Next to it is another tube that was covered with drywall. As you continue walking you enter another bedroom where the last tube is located. This is the bedroom where the worker in the tubes heard the pull chain toilet flush by itself.

As Carol went to get a flashlight for me so I could venture into the tubes, I did a small EVP session by myself in the tube. I said, "Hello! Is anybody here?" I could distinctly hear heavy breathing after I asked the questions.

The bedroom after the closet door was put back in its place. Notice the artwork on the wall is askew.
Author Photo

The door that leads to the bomb shelter inside the pump house tubes. *Author Photo*

CHAPTER 11

As we entered the tube we shined our flashlight down the tube, and at the end is a tiny door, which reminded me of something out of *Alice in Wonderland*. Carol told us that when they closed off the tubes her ex-husband turned part of the tube into a bomb shelter.

My husband and I ventured into the tube with only our phones and flashlights. After a few feet the tube is tall enough to stand in, and we eventually came to the point where all three tubes meet up. We walked through the door to the bomb shelter and on one side of the tube bunk beds and shelves were built. We found evidence of others having been there, as we saw an empty beer can. Eventually the tube comes to a dead end where it was sealed off with concrete so animals and transients would not be able to get in.

As my phone was recording EVPs my husband was taking photos. In the audio recordings throughout our journey into the tunnel you can hear phantom footsteps, as well as phantom breathing. At one point in my recording I asked my husband to shut the little door so I could take a few photos of the tube by myself. The door was closed and I made a note of how quiet it was in the bomb shelter part of the tube. There is a distinct, mysterious voice heard on my audio recording. I was unable to make out exactly what the voice was saying.

So there is no doubt in my mind that the tubes in the pump house are haunted. This is not at all shocking, considering that the Colorado River runs right alongside the building. One of the theories is that ghosts will use the energy from the running water to help manifest themselves. It is not uncommon to have an increase in paranormal activity around running water.

Part of the tube which was used as a bomb shelter. These shelves
were built to store food and supplies

TUBAC

Tubac is well-known today as an artist colony, but in 1752, when it was established, it was a major stop on the Camino Real, a path from Mexico to the settlements in California. Under constant attack from Apache Indians, it was abandoned in the 1840s.

My friend, Steve Hecksel, is fascinated with old mining towns and their history. He wrote the following chapter about the murder at Cerro Colorado, which is not far from Tubac.

MURDER AT CERRO COLORADO

Along the foothills of the Las Guijas Mountains, between the small communities of Arivaca and Amodo, is a lonely, dusty road less traveled. The road was once used as a thoroughfare between Sonora, Mexico, and the future Arizona Territory by Spanish explorers, the Apache, Mexican banditos, cattle ranchers, and miners seeking riches in gold and silver.

The foothills surrounding an unremarkable and relatively small mountain known as Cerro Colorado (Red Mountain) became a historically important mining community in the mid-eighteenth century. The lure of riches in gold, silver, and copper in this area attracted the attention of two ambitious brothers, Charles and John Poston, who developed the Heintzelman Mine.

Their little-known tale includes uplifting stories of exploring a new frontier, discovering a potential fortune in silver, promising political careers, and even a meeting with Abraham Lincoln. But beyond this story of discovery, wealth, and nation-building is one of untold dark human tragedy, including theft, torture, murder, grave robbing, lost treasure, and ghosts.

To set the scene, what is today Pima County, Arizona, was once land claimed by Mexico. The area around Cerro Colorado is just north of the small town of Arivaca. Arivaca (small springs) owes its roots to the Pima and Tohono O'odam Indians who lived in the area prior to the first exploration of Spanish explorers about 1695.

In 1833, a Mexican land grant created La Ariba Ranch, a sprawling 8,677-acre area for proposed cattle-grazing and farming. This ranch included the area where the Heintzelman Mine is, at the base of little Cerro Colorado Mountain, about twelve miles northwest of Arivaca.

In 1853, much of today's southern Arizona was purchased from Mexico by the United States as part of the Gadsden Purchase. In 1856, the ranch was sold to Charles and John Poston, two brothers from Kentucky who were originally lured to the western United States by riches fueled by the gold rush in California. The Poston brothers were assisted in their mining exploration by US Army Maj. Samuel Heintzelman, whom they had met on their way to the Arivaca area. Besides being the commander at Fort Yuma, Heintzelman was also an amateur geologist and a victim of gold fever. Maj. Heintzelman introduced the Poston brothers to a variety of financial investors from France and Cinncinati, Ohio, who funded both the purchase of the ranch and a search for mineral wealth.

The original mine, later called the Heintzelman, was named in honor of the man who had encouraged the brothers to search this area after hearing rumors of silver and gold previously collected by Native Americans and Spanish explorers. Heintzelman had confirmed the presence of silver on the ranch property after being led there a few years earlier by a Mexican teamster named Ouidican.

Heintzelman became partners with Charles and John Poston, who in 1856 formed the Sonora Exploring and Mining Company, with their headquarters in nearby Tubac. They invested $100,000 for several mining claims near Arivaca and the Santa Rita mountains. An interesting sidelight is that Samuel Colt, of Colt revolver fame, sat on the board of directors for the original company.

The Heintzelman mine and the area surrounding it was later referred to as Cerro Colorado based upon its proximity to the nearby modest mountain of the same name.

The mine was almost immediately a profitable silver producer, making in excess of $3,000 per day. The first run of ore through the mill yielded 2,287 ounces of silver and 300 pounds of copper. The main shaft was more than 120 feet deep and employed more than 200 workers. One silver nugget located in the mine weighed 56.25 pounds.

Charles, who was primary stockholder in the company, hired his brother John to be the on-site manager of the Heinzelman mine. This early success led Charles and his company to purchase additional mining claims in the area in the Santa Rita Mountains. Charles and brother John financed the construction of an adobe-walled small village containing several small houses and storage facilities for the miners to both live in and defend themselves from the Apaches and Mexican bandito raids. This walled community became know locally as Cerro Colorado.

The mining company hired a German mining engineer, Frederick Brucknow, to be responsible for the mineral exploration and physical construction of the mine. Frederick Brucknow later built a cabin southwest of Tombstone. Today the "Brucknow cabin" sits in ruins, but has extensive, well-documented notoriety as one of the most violent and bloody sites in southern Arizona history. During his ownership and successors, between 1860 and 1890, there were twenty-one murders documented, all connected to claim jumping, bandit home invasions, and Apache raids. Numerous unmarked graves reportedly still surround the cabin home site. The remains of the cabin are reportedly haunted by those souls who violently lost their lives there and whose restless spirits still seek revenge. Today, visitors at night report hearing muffled voices, bodiless footsteps, and faint gunshots, while others are sensitive to an overwhelming sense of dread. Some who decide to camp out in the vicinity of the original cabin are unable to complete an entire overnight's stay due to "unnatural activity."

By the middle of 1861, the success of the Heintzelman mine led to the construction of numerous small miner residences and supply buildings all surrounded by an adobe wall. This community was an outgrowth of the nearly 800–1,000 mining company employees working at the height of the mine's silver production. The majority of the miners were from Mexico.

Life was dangerous in this part of the country. Groups of outlaws from Mexico known locally as "banditos" raided north across the border to steal cattle and silver gold ore before heading back south and the safety of the border.

Racial tensions culminated in 1859, between Mexican ranch/mine employees from Sonora and Anglo-American local ranch/mine owners, leading to the bloody "Sonoita Massacre."

Apaches in the area were often bribed with food, tobacco, and supplies not to attack mining locations, the city of Tubac, and ranches. Periodic breeches in the fragile peace with the Apaches resulted in numerous atrocities initiated by both sides. Additional lack of security was caused by the US Army's decision to abandon Fort Buchanan (three miles southwest of present day Sonoita) due to lack of manpower from demands of the Civil War and Apache attacks. To add to the pain, logistical transportation issues led to shortages of key building materials, medicine, and consistent food supplies. It was the result of these conditions that Charles and John Poston constructed the protective walls around their outpost, Cerro Colorado.

It was during this period of turmoil surrounding Cerro Colorado that Charles Poston left the area for Washington, DC, after first appointing his brother John directly in charge of mining operations at the Heintzelman mine. Charles's main motivation for this move was to seek greater federal government protection for citizens, ranchers, and mine operators residing in this area later to be designated as the Arizona Territory.

He quickly renewed his contact with Gen. Heintzelman, who after the outbreak of the Civil War was transferred by the Union Army to the east. Charles received an appointment as a civilian aid to recently promoted Gen. Heintzelman. His ultimate goal was to obtain the official creation and designation of the Arizona Territory.

Charles lobbied members of Congress, where he focused on the importance of this area's vast, untapped mineral wealth to the success of a Union victory. In an attempt to secure a meeting with President Lincoln, Charles first secured a sample of silver directly from the Heintzelman mine and then contracted with Tiffany of New York to create an ornate $1,500.00 silver inkwell to personally present to the president.

Charles and others were ultimately successful in convincing the federal government to grant official territory status to Arizona in 1863. The following year Charles would be named the first delegate to the house of representatives and received the designation "Father of Arizona." But before the official designation came tragedy struck at Cerro Colorado. While working a section of the Heintzelman mine at a depth of about 120 feet, a tunnel suddenly collapsed. Initial rescue attempts involved digging laterally and vertically from adjacent tunnels, but both failed. After several days mine director John Poston and lead mining engineer Frederick Brucknow made the gut-wrenching conclusion that any further attempts to rescue the trapped miners were fruitless, and only further endangered the lives of those brave miners attempting the rescue. The trapped miners' fate was set: they would be permanently sealed in their pitch-black underground tomb. The death toll included an estimated fifteen to twenty Mexican and Native American miners.

Mining operations were shut down only long enough for the short-lived rescue attempt and a brief period of mourning. An additional problem then developed. Miners working in the mine tunnels close to the collapse during the next several weeks reported strange activity. Reports of audible faint, indistinguishable cries for help and tapping noises, combined with a sense of overwhelming dread, literally spooked the remaining primarily Mexican miners.

After a month or so of experiencing this activity, the Mexican miners simply refused to re-enter the mine and packed up and returned to Sonora. John Poston and Brucknow had difficulty locating local, experienced miners and searched for a solution. Brucknow, due to his Austrian/German heritage, was fortunately able to convince a group of veteran German miners to sign on with the company and re-enter the mine. The dangerous yet profitable work continued.

In this atmosphere danger lurked behind every hill, and the utter lack of real frontier law enforcement meant justice was often dealt out on the spot. At the end of 1861, John Poston, manager of the Heintzelman in the absence of his brother, was reviewing mining company production ledger books and noticed that something just was not right.

Profits were stagnant even as production increased, and reports from inside the mine were indicating a new promising silver strike at the 120-foot level. A mining foreman from Sonora named "Juanito" was caught stealing silver ore from the mine. The plot described said that during the week Juanito would skim high-grade silver ore from the daily production and then transport a portion of his proceeds in saddle bags back to his family's home in Sonora on his scheduled days off. During the week, while at the mine, he would bury it close by to avoid discovery.

One day Juanito was caught with silver ore-filled pockets. Upon hearing this news John Poston quickly called a meeting of mine employees. At this meeting, in front of numerous employees, John raised a rifle and shot and killed Juanito. It is speculated that John Poston took the law into his hands this day for a variety of reasons, but the most likely scenario is John, as manager of the mine, had a position of authority to uphold as awarded by his brother and heavily depended on the honesty of each and every one of his employees. The court system could take months to play out, and the company could ill afford the loss of silver through dishonest employees. A quick "solution" would prop up his position of authority.

Only after the killing of Juanito did the details of his plot come in to clearer perspective and a lost treasure legend was born. If Juanito buried his proceeds and only periodically delivered them to Sonora, then where and how much silver is quietly, patiently waiting under the sandy soil near the mine? Treasure hunters speculate that Juanito would not have ventured far from the mine to bury the silver due to the ever present danger of the Apache and to avoid bringing attention to himself. Ever since the killing of Juanito, hopeful, intrepid treasure hunters have scoured the desert hills and dry, sandy washes around the mine, hoping to locate the estimated $70,000.00 (1861 value) worth of silver ore.

Tragedy hit a second time in 1861, and this time it was personal. The killing of Juanito ignited a firestorm chain of events. Juanito had friends in Sonora—not the kind you brag about, but the kind that called themselves banditos. Shortly after his killing a group of banditos decided to ride up from Sonora to Cerro Colorado to rob the mine of its silver and seek revenge for Juanito's death.

The plan was launched. The night before the banditos reached the mine the group camped on the property of a ranch about ten miles directly south. The ranch owner sent a rider to notify John Poston and his employees of the presence of this group. Even though the events that followed get a bit foggy, one thing is for sure: John Poston and his German miners were ready and prepared for the prospect of the banditos' arrival. According to those who survived the events of the following day, John designated a few of his men to bury their current pile of valuable silver ore. Based upon their current level of ore production, it is estimated that about $30,000.00 (1861 value) worth of silver was buried. Due to their lack of time and the risk of discovery by local Apaches the ore was most likely buried in close proximity.

The Banditos were far superior in weaponry and quickly gained control of the adobe-walled village by late morning. Reportedly at least two German miners were shot and killed and several more were wounded during the initial attack. The leader of the banditos now turned his full attention to John Poston.

The demand made was for the miners to turn over all of the silver ore and the silver ore allegedly buried by Juanito. John Poston refused to divulge any information on the location of the silver ore, even under threat of torture. His refusal to cooperate cost him his life, as before the banditos left the compound John Poston was dead. After most likely taking some money and the personal possessions of the remaining miners and damaging or hauling off most of the mine equipment, the banditos started their escape back to Sonora. The legend concerning the buried ore is that the specific location died with John Poston and it is still out there. Two buried treasure legends based around one specific mine.

The news of the attack on Cerro Colorado reached the city of Tubac within hours. Charles Poston, who had recently returned from the east coast to visit his mining company headquarters, heard the news and immediately headed for Cerro Colorado accompanied by Frederick Brucknow and a few others. When they arrived, Charles quickly learned that his brother was dead. Charles, Frederick Brucknow, and a few miners loaded John's body on to a wagon and proceeded to the city of Arivaca, about nine miles distant. Charles helped bury his own brother in Cerro Colorado Cemetery on the outskirts of town.

The history of the Heintzelman mine did not end with the murder of John Poston. Over the years the mine has sporadically re-opened, but also suffered many

Detail of the memorial of John Lee
Poston in deserted Cerro Colorado.
Author Photo

setbacks. During a fifteen-year period (1863–1878), roving bands of Apache created unsafe conditions for sustained mining operations.

In 1901, there was another cave in a tunnel that resulted in the death of at least one Mexican miner. The events of World War I, the Great Depression era, World War II, and recently stricter environmental regulations have all had a stifling effect on profitable operation. Today all active mining operations have ceased, but there are still active, privately owned mining claims in the immediate area.

Today the Heintzelman mine is a quiet, lonely place. The beautiful desert scenery belies its violent past. There are scattered remnants of stone walls, cement foundations, wood clapboard, broken glass, and several fenced off, partially collapsed mine entrances. Caution needs to be exercised around all mine entrances, and because some of the tunnels in this area were not deep, subsidence or even collapse from ground level is a potential danger.

For the curious visitor there is one remnant of the past that is hard to miss. On the side of a gravel road sits a concrete monument that at first glance looks like an above-ground tomb. Many recent articles written on Cerro Colorado or the Heintzelman mine attribute this monument as the burial site of John Poston, but further research has revealed a different answer.

As previously discussed, there was a tunnel collapse in 1901. The miners buried the Mexican miner under a concrete slab and constructed the original above-ground crypt. Treasure hunters over the years have damaged the monument looking for treasure, thinking that the monument is the burial site for John Poston. A sinister turn occurred within the first few years after the burial, when the entire body was stolen from the crypt in a further attempt to locate the treasure, a treasure map, or simply to rob any valuables originally buried with the unnamed miner.

During the 1980s, a great-great-grandson of John Poston visited the Cerro Colorado area and decided this monument would be the perfect place to insert a plaque to honor him, inscribing his name and the years of his life, 1830–1861. This act further perpetuated the incorrect impression that this is the official burial site for John Poston.

The area surrounding Cerro Colorado and the mine hides the spirits of those who lost their lives here, whether searching for riches or the victims of crime. A modern wooden plaque placed next to the concrete monument that honored John Poston is now missing but describes the scene well:

HERE LIES, SOME SAY, ARIVACA JOHN.
KILLED HIM A THIEF, AND NOW HE'S GONE.
THE COMPANY'S SILVER, HE VOWED TO SAVE.
BUT ALL HE GOT WAS AN EARLY GRAVE.
MEXICAN OUTLAWS DONE HIM IN.
NEVER TO ROAM, THESE PARTS AGAIN.

Memorial of John Lee Poston.
Author Photo

References:

Desert Magazine, September 1948: "Haunted Silver," p. 6–9.

Green Valley News, 2/10/13, "Cerro Colorado."

Southern Arizona News/Examiner, 9/23/15, "Traces Remain of Poston Brothers."

Dillon, Richard H. (1999). "Poston, Charles Debrille." In Garraty, John A.; Carnes, Mark C. *American national Biography*. New York: Oxford University Press. pp. 735–6.

Sherman, James E; Barbara H. Sherman (1969). *Ghost Towns of Arizona*. University of Oklahoma Press.

ArizonaExperience.com: "Charles D. Poston, Father of Arizona."

ExperienceAZ.com: "Arivaca Adventure."

GVHC Library File #26, Heintzelman Mine.

ThePhoenixEnigma.com, 12/18/15, "Charles Poston."

An abandoned mine shaft in Cerro Colorado. *Author Photo*

CHAPTER 13
BISBEE'S EVERGREEN CEMETERY

Bisbee's Evergreen Cemetery was established in 1912, to replace Bisbee's original cemetery, which is now City Park in Old Bisbee (see my chapter about City Park in *Southern Arizona's Most Haunted*).

I decided to add this bonus chapter for those readers who wish to visit the graves of a few of the people mentioned in this book.

If you do venture into Evergreen Cemetery, please be respectful of the graves and the families who have loved ones buried there.

Bisbee's Evergreen Cemetery

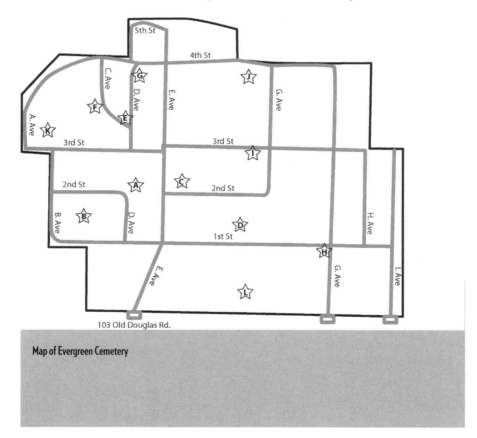

Map of Evergreen Cemetery

A - Kay Ross

The burial plot of Kay Ross, his wife, and child. *Author Photo*

B - Arthur Lewis (unmarked grave)

Arthur Lewis's unmarked grave. *Author Photo*

D - Constance Hoover

Baby Constance Hoover's grave.
Author Photo

E - Charles & Micheal McColloch

The burial plot of Charles and Michael McCulloch. *Author Photo*

F - Dale Duke

Dale Duke's grave.
Author Photo

G - Jean Diane Mitchel
(from my first book *Southern
Arizona's Most Haunted*)

The grave of Jeanne Diane Mitchell
and her parents (from *Southern
Arizona's Most Haunted*).
Author Photo

H - James Busk

The grave of James A. Busk.
Author Photo

I - J. C. Tappenier
(first person shot during the Bisbee Massacre
from *Southern Arizona's Most Haunted*. In an
unmarked grave in the Howell plot)

J. C. Tappenier in an unmarked
grave in the Howell Plot (from
Southern Arizona's Most Haunted).
Author Photo

CHAPTER 13

J - Carlos Calderon (unmarked grave)

Unmarked grave of Carlos Calderon.
Author Photo

K - Modesto Vastido (on his death certificate and headstone his name appears as Modesto Bastidas)

The grave of Modesto Vastido. *Author Photo*

L – Frank Valencia

The grave of Frank Valencia. *Author Photo*

RENEE grew up in the suburbs of Philadelphia in a haunted house. She spent her childhood hiding under the covers, too scared to see what was looming over her. She attended Otis College of Art and Design in Los Angeles and graduated with a BFA in toy design. During her college years, she became fascinated with folklore, which lead her to start collecting ghost stories. In 2007, she moved to Bisbee, Arizona, and started the Old Bisbee Ghost Tour. Soon after, she started her second successful business Sweet Midnight, selling products "on the darker side of cute." The Bisbee Chamber of Commerce awarded Renee the title of The Official Ambassador to the Ghosts and Spirits of Bisbee for her work in preserving the local ghost stories and their rich history. Renee resides in Bisbee with her menagerie of pets and her hubby.